GO SEE PEOPLE

Grow Your Fundraising Program

by

Joseph Tumolo, CAP®

Go See People

Grow Your Fundraising Program

By Joseph Tumolo, CAP®

Copyright © 2017 Joseph Tumolo

Published by SkillBites Publishing

All Rights Reserved.

ISBN-10: 1-942489-32-3

ISBN-13: 978-1-942489-32-0

To my sweet Lorraine. Your support and love never go unnoticed.

TABLE OF CONTENTS

Dedication..iii

Preface...vii

Introduction..1

SECTION I: MINDSET   3

Chapter 1:   *The Power of Training* *5*

Chapter 2:   *Get Your Head Straight* *11*

Chapter 3:   *Think Big*...*17*

Chapter 4:   *What's Your Money Story?* *23*

Chapter 5:   *The Right Approach*............................*29*

Chapter 6:   *Abundance Mentality* *39*

Chapter 7:   *Give and Get* *43*

Chapter 8:   *Choice Management*...........................*51*

Chapter 9:   *Be the Eternal Student* *57*

Chapter 10:   *Smile*...*61*

Chapter 11:   *Gratitude* *65*

SECTION II: BEHAVIOR   69

Chapter 12: *Goal Setting*..*71*

Chapter 13: *Track Results and Behavior*............................*75*

Chapter 14: *Test*..*85*

Chapter 15: *Write It Down* *91*

Chapter 16: *The Rule of Threes* *95*

Chapter 17: *Planning* *99*

Chapter 18: *Clarity*... *105*

SECTION III: SKILLSETS   109

Chapter 19: *Adapting Your Style*.................................. *111*

Chapter 20: *Listening*.. *119*

Chapter 21: *Asking Better Questions* *127*

Chapter 22: *Getting the Visit* *133*

Chapter 23: *What's Your Message?*................................ *141*

Chapter 24: *Making the Ask* *149*

Chapter 25: *Help People Decide* *153*

Chapter 26: *Clear Future* *157*

Chapter 27: *Choose Your Words Carefully* *161*

Chapter 28: *Follow Up and Follow Through* *167*

Chapter 29: *Pick Up the Check*.. *171*

Chapter 30: *A Thank You Would Be Nice*........................ *173*

Chapter 31: *Final Thoughts*... *177*

PREFACE

Upon receiving an award for raising more money than anyone else in the organization, Fred was asked, "How did you raise so much?" Fred's simple response was, "I went out and saw people." Wow, is that all it takes to get better results and close more gifts? Well, not completely, but it's a great start. So much of this book is based on the simple premise that we get much better results when we spend more time out of the office with donors and prospects. Activity begets more activity. The more of the right activity we do, the more good stuff happens. That being said, we do need to make sure we are spending that time with the right people and using the time in a way that's most beneficial to our organization and to our donors. This book will show you how to do that.

I speak to fundraisers all over the country. In the last fifteen years, I have spoken to thousands. Time and again I hear one of three things:

People tell me they just are not spending enough time visiting donors. Others tell me they are trying to get in front of donors, but it's hard to get donors to agree to a visit. Still others say they are getting in front of donors, but it's more difficult than ever to get them to make a commitment.

The good news is there are ways to get in front of more donors on a consistent basis. It's all about reevaluating the choices we make each day, continually honing our communication and relationship skills while being deliberate about spending more time with donors.

I have spent the last thirty-three years selling and managing salespeople—the last fifteen of those years in the fundraising world helping organizations build major and planned giving programs and as a part-time frontline major and planned gifts officer. The ideas and methodology in this book come from many years of testing and trying different approaches. My approach is based on relationship selling. Great relational fundraisers are just like great relational salespeople. They make the right choices each day. They plan. They set, track, and exceed their goals. They always do what is right for the client or donor, even if that means not making the sale or getting the gift. They continually hone their communication and relationship skills. And like researchers, they evaluate everything they are doing to see what produces the greatest results. Those who follow the methodology spelled out here all tell me they are spending more time with better qualified donors. And by doing so, they are closing more and larger outright and deferred gifts.

INTRODUCTION

Many years ago, I started working with my business coach, Bruce. Bruce challenged me to think differently. He would suggest ways for me to change the way I was thinking and doing things. My immediate reaction was to resist. I resisted because it did not immediately make sense to me. Bruce would get so mad, yelling, "Stop resisting; figure out how I am right." It took me a few months to realize that I had the tendency to resist ideas, people, anything that did not immediately match what I was used to. My wife might say, "Let's go to the opera." My immediate reaction would have been, "No thanks. I am not sitting through three hours of boring music and people singing in a language I do not understand." I did not even give it a chance, nor did I consider how my wife felt when I so quickly turned away from what she wanted. Someone might recommend a superhero movie. My first reaction was, "I am not sitting through two hours of mindless special effects." Again, I didn't even give it a chance.

I did that with music, restaurants, business ideas, and more. Gradually I developed the skillset of suspending disbelief—the skillset of not being so quick to dismiss someone or something. The skillset to say, "How does that make sense? How is that person right? What is the value in that? So many people are attracted to that, so what is there that I am not giving a chance?" I have enjoyed and learned so many new things by taking that approach. I even love going to the opera.

So, with this book, I encourage you to give thought to the ideas I present here. I don't have all the answers. Not everything may make sense to you immediately or ever. Read it with an open mind. What have you stopped doing that you should start doing again? What do you already know but are not doing? There is a difference between what we know and what we do. Are you doing what you know? What can you change, improve, or adjust?

I hope this book gives you new insights and tools you can use to take your fundraising to the next level and improve the quality of your relationships and your life.

SECTION I:
MINDSET

I was cleaning out my basement recently and found an old suitcase that I got when I graduated college. It gave me pause to stop and think about how long I have had that suitcase and how much of life I have lived since then. It also made me think about my mental baggage—all the thoughts and feelings I have been carrying with me my whole life. Like that old suitcase, that mental baggage is always there. Sometimes it's tucked away, and I forget it's there until something happens and it resurfaces. A lot of my mental baggage centers around my need for approval, to be liked by everyone. I am aware of it, I have come to accept it, and I am getting better at recognizing it when it surfaces and at dealing with it in a healthy way.

It's assumed that we are all adults and that everyone is perfectly adjusted in life. The reality is that we all have mental baggage, but few people discuss it in public, let alone in the workplace. Having the right mindset is a big component of being successful in life and business. This means being aware of and dealing with our mental baggage and negative emotions as they arise. Developing and maintaining the right mindset takes practice like any other skillset. Sales and self-help guru Zig Ziglar used to say that having a positive attitude and learning positive self-talk is like brushing your teeth. You don't do it once and then forget about it. It needs to be part of your daily routine. It takes practice.

This section will help you develop or adjust your mindset to a more positive, peaceful, and effective one.

CHAPTER 1:

THE POWER OF TRAINING

"My land, the power of training! Of influence! Of education! It can bring a body up to believe anything."

– Mark Twain

You may have heard the statistic that the average gift officer stays in his or her job less than two years. How can relationships be built with donors when gift officers don't stay around long enough? Fundraisers move on for all sorts of reasons, such as better pay elsewhere, burnout, general unhappiness, and poor performance. But what can we do to improve employee retention in the nonprofit sector?

Dan Pink, author of the bestselling book *Drive: The Surprising Truth About What Motivates Us*, writes that what employees really want is:

- *Autonomy*—the chance to be self-directed and independent at work;

- *Mastery*—the chance to be good at what they do, over-coming challenges and finding creative solutions; and

- *Purpose*—the chance to feel they are contributing to the greater good, to be driven from within to work toward a larger group goal.

Let's focus on the second want, Mastery. When people get stuck, when they don't seem to grow, when their fundraising revenue is flat, it's often a result of doing the same things they have always done. They are stuck in the weeds. They don't have an objective observer to help them see things from a higher level.

So few for-profit and nonprofit organizations have structured training programs. If you are leading fundraisers, then I encourage you to develop or evaluate your training program. Effective training is about developing new habits. Sending your gift officers to a one-day seminar once or twice a year is not structured training. Consider outsourcing your training. I hear that Joe Tumolo guy is pretty good…

Training is not just for newbies. Training should be a part of everyone's regimen, no matter how long he or she has been in the field. Structured and consistent training reinforced with one-on-one coaching will get you and your team to the next level much faster and much more sustainably than everyone figuring it out as they go along. There is a myth that most fundraisers have had proper training in order to have the experience they have. The reality is that most fundraisers have learned on the job with very little guidance or mentoring. I hear time and time again from people: "Oh, I had no formal training, so I had to figure it out on my own." There is a better way!

Getting to the next level in any job, sport, or activity requires continually learning new ways to be more effective and practicing what is learned over and over with intention. Training is about developing new habits, and doing so takes time. The latest research shows that it takes at least sixty-six days to develop new habits.[1] Proper training is not about giving the student all the answers. Learning comes about when the student struggles. It's in that struggle that the student discovers the answers for themselves. Proper training is about testing what is learned in the real world, then returning back to the classroom to continually hone those skills.

An ongoing training program that's customized to fit the preferences and styles of each of your team members will improve performance, show your staff that you are invested in them, and ultimately lead to better job satisfaction. In my years of working with fundraisers of all experience levels, I have seen the power of training change behavior and improve results. Here are a few examples.

Mary was having difficulty finding the time to pick up the phone to call donors. She kept saying she was too busy. After all, she had three special events a year, and her marketing person was on maternity leave. She convinced herself and those around her that getting out to see donors on a consistent basis was impossible. Mary and I worked

---

1. Phillippa Lally et. al., "How habits are formed: Modelling habit formation in the real world," *Eur. J. Soc. Psychol.* 40 (2010): 998–1009, doi: 10.1002/ejsp.674.

together to determine what she had to give up in order to have more time to make the calls. We implemented a call tracking system to help her set a goal for the number of calls she needed to make and to track those calls. Mary learned how to develop a new mindset and belief system that helped her realize she had more time than she thought. She learned a new methodology for increasing her volume of calls. This led to more visits and larger gifts from her donors.

Dwight was making donor calls but complained that no one wanted to visit with him. He was miserable and his performance review reflected that. After a training course Dwight attended on getting the visit, I worked with Dwight to create a calling script outline. Through role-playing, he developed a concise, compelling message that increased his success rate of getting the visit by over 30 percent.

Cindy was doing well getting in front of donors. She was "mentioning" planned giving as an option for her donors to consider, but never really got around to making the ask. I worked with Cindy to move away from her agenda and to instead focus on the donor's agenda. As my friend Brian Sagrestano likes to say, "Donor-centered philanthropy is helping the donor accomplish what they want first, then matching that with the needs of our organization and those we serve." After months of continual coaching and adjusting, Cindy was able to focus on the donor's agenda first, then hers. She found that when she left her agenda in the car, she had much more meaningful conversations with donors. She grew more comfortable inviting donors to join her as a member of the planned giving society. Her legacy society membership increased over 50 percent in the first year.

Karen had no system in place for managing her prospects. Months would go by and she would find herself making just a handful of donor calls. She had a few substantial conversations with donors, but they never seemed to go anywhere. Life would take over and she would often forget to follow up with those donors. Karen and I worked together to develop a qualified prospect pool and created a donor relation management system with a strategy for each of her donors, along with clear timelines of next steps for each donor. Her monthly visits doubled as a result, and her revenue is growing every year.

 IF YOU REMEMBER NOTHING ELSE:

✓ Don't ask, "What if I spend money training my staff and they leave?" Ask yourself, "What if I don't and they stay?"

CHAPTER 2:

GET YOUR HEAD STRAIGHT

So much of success in all areas of life comes down to developing the right mindset and belief system. Much of the training that I see focuses strictly on skillsets. Continually improving our skillsets is critical to our success, but it's just a part of the equation. Developing a higher level of self-awareness of who we are, how our past has defined us, and how we think is equally valuable.

Let's face it. We all need to keep a good face with our bosses, coworkers, donors, and so on. Talking about our feelings, worries, and concerns is not "good for business." Everyone is expected to have his or her act together. At the same time, we all have our mental baggage, or "head trash," as I like to call it.

According to a study completed at the University of California, Riverside, our personalities stay pretty much the same throughout our lives, starting in our early childhood years and continuing until the day we die. The results showed that personality traits observed in children as young as first graders were strong predictors of adult behavior. "We remain recognizably the same person," said study author Christopher Nave. "This speaks to the importance of understanding personality because it does follow us wherever we go across time and contexts."[2]

Here are some common examples of mental baggage and how it affects people in the workplace.

- As children, wanting to please our parents, we develop a high need for approval. As adults, that high need for approval can prevent us from speaking our minds when something bothers us for fear of not being liked by others. As managers, our need for approval can prevent us from addressing an issue with an employee because we want them to like us.

- Fear of confrontation. This is a big one. I have heard many business owners and managers complain about a staff person repeatedly, but never confront the employee to get a resolution. Instead of sitting down with the person and dealing with the issues, they carry resentment for the person. This can make for a very toxic workplace environment. Respectful confrontation leads to resolution and happier, more productive employees.

- Lack of control. We all have control freaks in our lives. Without getting into an area I am not qualified to write about, it's obvious that this trait is developed in childhood. A perfect example of a control freak in

2 Live Science, August 6, 2010.

action is often found in what we call "Founder's Syndrome". Sadly, many non-profits never reach their full potential because well-meaning CEOs or founders on organizations won't let go and trust others to try new approaches.

But wait, there is hope. We can reshape our thinking, eliminate negative thoughts, and retrain our brains to think in new ways. Let's look at this from a fundraising perspective. Growing our fundraising program by 10-15 percent each year is good. To then grow our program by 25 percent, 50 percent, or more requires us to change the way we behave, act, and think. It requires that we think bigger and develop a higher sense of abundance and gratitude. This higher level of thinking requires us to throw out the old way of thinking small. We must ignore that little voice that says "that's impossible, it will never work, remember what happened last time".

Sometimes we need a complete thinking overhaul, but other times our thinking just needs to be tweaked. Little changes can lead to bigger wins.

Matt Parker is a sports performance specialist. He has helped lots of champions like Great Britain's Olympic cycling team and England's Rugby team make minor adjustments to achieve greater success. Parker, and many other sports performance pros, discovered that once someone gets to a certain level of performance, the rate at which they improve slows down. We have all experienced that. Anytime we start learning a new skillset, we tend to learn fast because we are starting at zero. Then once we reach a level of success, the rate at which we learn and improve decreases.

I learned this from studying the guitar. When I started out I was improving at a fast pace. Learning to strum chords and understand basic music theory came quickly (with a lot of practice). But then I hit a plateau. Playing more complex jazz chords and improvising seemed to bring my progress to a screeching halt. For months I kept ordering online guitar courses that promised to simplify learning the guitar, but I came to realize there is no fast way. Getting to the next level in my playing is coming slowly, but it's the little steps I take each day that gradually make me a better player. This applies to so many activities in our personal and professional life.

Quick Tip

Are you frustrated by what you perceive as a lack of progress with a particular skillset or your favorite hobby? Try this mantra: "This is a journey with no destination." I repeat it every time I feel like I am not making progress.

Sometimes a little tweak in our behavior can help get us off the plateau. In 2008, Parker worked with the Great Britain Olympic cycling team, certainly well experienced and accomplished riders. According to an interview with *The Independent,* on Parker's suggestion, the team made some minor adjustments to their training and riding that included consuming large quantities of fish oil and cherries, spraying alcohol on their tires to remove dirt and increase stickiness, and several others. These little changes, which many other teams overlooked, helped the team win eight Olympic Gold medals. Parker's research showed him two things. First, getting to the next level when you are already at a high level requires small, subtle changes. Second, getting to the next level is a gradual, slow process. Parker calls it marginal gains.[3]

So how do we apply this concept to our work in fundraising? For those of us who have been doing this work for a while, it's not so easy to make big improvements in a short amount of time. Incorporating the principles that Parker and his contemporaries have tested, we too can make minor adjustments to achieve marginal gains that in time will make us some of the best relationship builders and fundraisers in the world!

Here are a few examples of minor adjustments that I have found to improve my results. We'll explore these in more detail later in the book.

- Developing, practicing, and delivering more concise and compelling voicemails and e-mails.

- Never inviting anyone to a meeting without at least a three-point agenda.

- Following up board member conversations with an e-mail of what was discussed and any action steps to be taken.

---

3. http://www.independent.co.uk/sport/olympics/cycling/ head-of-marginal-gains-helps-gb-gold-machine-stay-in-front-8010110.html

- Implementing a better system for following up with people.

- Keeping a "lessons learned" journal. Every time something doesn't go as planned, figure out why, write it in the journal, and review it on a quarterly basis. "We win or we learn."

 IF YOU REMEMBER NOTHING ELSE:

✓ Our personalities are developed at an early age. How does that affect the way you fundraise?

✓ It's not always big changes that make the most difference.

✓ Success is a journey, not a destination.

CHAPTER 3:

THINK BIG

"Think big and don't listen to people who tell you it can't be done. Life is too short to think small."

– Tim Ferriss

We all tend to think too small. Growing up, your parents may have told you to be practical, be level headed, don't go too crazy with your thinking because you are sure to be disappointed. Or maybe you have been doing the same type of work, perhaps for different charities, and getting similar results for many years. Not bad results, but not extraordinary results either. Somewhere along the way, we lose our ability to think and dream big. It is human nature to limit our thinking about what's possible based on our past experiences.

There is a great story about a man named Roger Bannister. He was the first runner ever to break the four-minute-mile threshold in 1954. Prior to that day, everyone said it could not be done. What's really interesting is that within just forty-six days, Bannister's record was broken by his rival John Landy. Others followed soon after. We base our perception of what's possible based on what we or others have done in the past.

I learned this when I started getting serious about running years ago. I was stuck at running 5K races for years. It was not until I ran in the famous Philadelphia Broad Street ten-mile run that I learned that so much of what held me back was my self-limiting beliefs. I could not visualize running more than a 5K. Eventually, I went on to complete a half Ironman triathlon, something I never would have thought possible based on my old belief system. I was by no means an athletic person (at least that was the story I made up and repeatedly told myself). Now I know I can do so much more than I ever dreamed possible. Ultra-marathoner Dean Karnazes has run 350 miles nonstop. Does Dean think small? That's a big negatory, good buddy.

As a young sales guy in the 80s, working in the family printing and direct mail business, the thought of making $100,000 seemed far out of reach. I did not have the belief system that I could sell enough to earn that much in commissions. So, I played it safe and focused on selling smaller accounts. Eventually I grew my client base to lots of small accounts and made a very nice living. Once I passed that $100,000 level, it became second nature. Managing a lot of small accounts, however, was driving me crazy. After fifteen years of that mindset and doing business that way, we sold our family business to a large, billion-dollar company. For the first time, I was in a large office with over thirty salespeople. Most of those men and women built their book of business selling to large national accounts. After all, it often takes just as much time to sell a large account as it does to sell a small one, and the payoffs are much higher. After a few months of hanging out with these think-big folks, I started to change my thinking and my focus. I started pursuing large national accounts for the first time in my life. It was not long before I landed a large national account that increased my income by over 45 percent that year. Just like that triathlon experience, I learned I could do so much more. The only thing holding me back was my self-limiting belief.

Exercise: Take a moment now to think of an area in your life where you are thinking small. Where did that thinking come from? Who told you that doing more could not be done? What specific action can you take to change that?

We've all heard the stories of brilliant inventors like Marconi and Tesla who were way ahead of their time. People thought they were crazy. Is that what's holding you back? The fear of failure? The fear that others will think you are incompetent because you are not (in their minds) thinking clearly or playing it safe? I fully recognize that when you must answer to leadership and your board you have to be careful with what you promise, but there is a difference between what you promise and dreaming big.

Abraham Lincoln said, "The best way to predict the future is to create it." So, create the future you want. Dream it up. Think bigger.

Exercise: Look at your goals for your fundraising program this year. Do they look achievable? Do they excite you and drive you? Now take one goal. Let's say you have a goal to increase your annual fund by 15 percent this year. Okay, it's a decent goal, most likely attainable. Now let's pretend you set a goal to increase it by 100 percent. Yes, 100 percent. What's your first reaction to that premise? Probably "that's impossible." And why does that seem impossible? Because you are basing your thinking on past experience. Do you think that no one in the history of fundraising has ever doubled his or her fundraising revenue in one year? Plenty have, I am sure. The past does not predict the future. So, suspend disbelief and then ask yourself, how can I do that? How can I double my fundraising revenue in one year? Take out a legal pad. Write that question at the top of the page and number the lines vertically down the page from one to twenty. Now, start brainstorming twenty ways that you could double your annual fund revenue this year. Don't qualify your ideas. Just write them down. There are no wrong answers. Don't stop until you write down twenty ideas. If you get stuck, write something silly—just keep writing. The key with this exercise, and all brainstorming exercises, is to just keep thinking of things to keep the flow going. Once you stop, you are more likely to get stuck. Here are six examples of brainstorming ideas (remember, there are no bad ideas):

How can I double my fundraising program this year?

1. Ask every donor to double their giving this year.

2. Double the amount of time I am spending with donors every week.

3. Find a donor to create a Challenge Ask.

4. Sit down with every board member and ask them to introduce me to three people who might be open to learning more about our program.

5. Present this question to twenty-five of my top donors. Tell them I want to double our fundraising this year and ask them how they would do that if they were me.

6. Set a fundraising goal for my top 150 donors.

Get the idea? You'll be amazed at what you come up with. Now—and this is key—take three of the twenty ideas and implement them within thirty days. That's how you start thinking bigger and getting bigger results, my friend!

"For more about thinking big, see Chapter 12: Goal Setting"

Exercise: Keep a negative thought journal. According to scientists, we have 60,000 thoughts a day. What's alarming is that 80 percent of those thoughts are negative. Psychiatrist Dr. Daniel Amen reports that most of those negative thoughts are habitual. They are the same thoughts we have carried with us our entire lives. He calls them ANTs (Automatic Negative Thoughts). By being aware of them, we can then begin to change the negative thoughts to positive ones.

I keep a negative thought journal. Every time I find myself with a negative thought, I write it in my journal. Knowing that I have to record my negative thoughts makes me acutely aware of my thoughts throughout the day. I now catch myself a lot sooner when I start to think a negative thought, and I release it before I get sucked into the negative vortex. Negative thoughts include fear, worry, shame, pessimism, jealousy, anger, sadness, and many more! Try it for a week and see if you don't find yourself reducing your amount of negative thoughts.

IF YOU REMEMBER NOTHING ELSE:

✓ Squash those ANTs. Be aware of your thoughts and change the negative ones to positive.

✓ The amount of money you are making or raising is directly proportionate to your belief system. Change your belief system. Think bigger!

CHAPTER 4:

WHAT'S YOUR MONEY STORY?

"Money can't buy you happiness, but it can buy you a yacht big enough to pull up right alongside it."
— David Lee Roth

Considering we are in the business of raising money, it's important to understand our personal story around money and how that story could affect the way we fundraise. A great question to ask yourself is, "How much is a lot of money?" As a young sales kid out of college, I had a limited view of how much a lot of money was. I remember it like it was yesterday. My sales trainer, Harry Powers, told me, "Joe, you are making exactly how much you think you are worth and not a penny more." Harry was right. As a straight-commission salesperson, a good portion of how much I made was tied to how much I thought I was worth. I did not see myself as a several hundred thousand dollar a year salesperson, so I hung out in my comfort zone. Certainly, I made a nice living, but my income could have been much more had I believed I was capable of making more.

When I got into fundraising, I noticed my concept of money was affecting my confidence in asking donors to increase their giving. As a disclaimer, I would never suggest pressuring or even asking a donor to give more than they are able and feel good about giving. But, as a donor and fundraiser, I see gift officers not asking donors for enough because of their own limited beliefs.

Ask yourself this question. How much is a lot of money? What is your perception of a large gift? What do your board and leadership consider a major gift? What would happen if you increased that threshold? What would have to change in your organization? My guess is that the first thing that needs changing is everyone's mindset.

Another money story that I created for myself was that people with wealth are different, that they deserve to be treated differently than everyone else. I resented those who had more money than I had, instead of being happy for their success and understanding that the vast majority of people with wealth earned it. I was intimidated by wealthy people. It took me a long time to understand that they were just like me, only they were willing to take more chances. They were willing to make more sacrifices and maybe trade some leisure time with working time. It's only money. When we breathe our final breath, the money will mean nothing. Our relationships and the good we did with our resources will be all that matters.

I have had the pleasure of meeting with Jay Cherney on several occasions. Jay is a psychologist with many years of experience in clinical and private practice. Jay's current focus is working with high-net-worth individuals. He works with donors and their families to help them sort through the psychological aspects of having wealth, giving it away, and all the family dynamics that go with it. Most high-net-worth individuals have lots of professional advisors to help them through the legal and tax implications, but very few have advisors who talk about what's going on psychologically and emotionally with them and their families.

In our personal correspondence, Cherney wrote:

Why is it so hard to talk about money? People become uncomfortable when the topic of money arises because it is very personal and makes us feel vulnerable. Our money stories are often formed at an early age by watching those around us. They reveal our core values, emotions, and needs. Money stories drive most of our decisions, even though we're usually not conscious of them. Cherney shared that when he was young, he lost five dollars. He said that at the time, it was a "life catastrophe." His mother chewed him out, leading him to believe that money was precious and had to be guarded.

It took Jay a long time to realize that event had stayed with him his entire life. Jay says he hasn't forgotten it, but he has learned to catch himself before he starts his old money story.

We all have stories our parents told us about money. Let me preface this by saying that my parents' generation and their parents grew up in very different times. For instance, my grandparents grew up during the Depression, so it's completely understandable how they would have a very different story around money than the next generation and beyond. It is not my intent to say our parents or grandparents were wrong; God knows most worked and sacrificed a lot more than I have. My intent is to make you aware of stories that may still be lying beneath the surface and having an effect, maybe a not so obvious one, on your concept of money and how you approach fundraising.

Some of the more popular ideas around money that the Depression and World War II generation taught us include:

"Money does not grow on trees." Yes, but this phrase makes it sound like money is scarce. We need to have an abundance mentality to be successful at raising money. There are plenty of people (donors) who have money, all of whom will give it away to the right charity if asked at the right time, in the right manner, and for the right purpose.

"It's not polite to talk to people about money." This is a big one. We wouldn't stay employed for very long if we did not talk to people about money. I do believe in respecting donors' rights to privacy. I would never want to make a donor feel uncomfortable while talking about money. The best way to find out is to ask them how they feel about money and giving it away.

"The rich keep getting richer." Okay, this one has some political undertones, well beyond the purpose and scope of this book. Whatever your political beliefs, I would encourage you to view this statement as negative. If the rich keep getting richer and they are charitable, isn't that a good thing?

"The love for money is the root of all evil." This one comes from the Bible, 1 Timothy 6:10. Mark Twain once said, "The lack of money is the root of all evil." Yes, the love for money is not healthy, but being driven to make money to an end and doing good things with it enables the nonprofit sector to do what it does.

If you grew up in a household with little wealth, do you have a scarcity mentality that may cause you to hesitate when asking for the big gifts? If your money story is one of generosity, then you may have a hard time empathizing with someone who is hesitant to make what you consider to be an appropriately sized gift. Seeing both sides of the coin helps you maintain a healthy attitude toward money and frees you up to be the best fundraiser you can be.

Exercise: Here is a simple gesture you can do to maintain a healthy attitude with money: over-tip. I started giving a $20 tip once a week to someone in the service industry who was not expecting a tip, or not one of that size. It could be the person drying your car off at the car wash or the server at your favorite breakfast spot. What is even more interesting is to over-tip someone who is not pleasant or providing great service. That's not easy; for me it takes more effort and requires a deeper level of compassion. Who knows what hardship that server may be going through? There could be a good reason why they are not smiling or are even being rude.

IF YOU REMEMBER NOTHING ELSE:

✓ Your money story influences the way you fundraise. If you don't know your money story, figure it out. Then rewrite it so it's healthy and helps you be your best.

✓ A small gift to your organization could feel like a large gift to your donor.

CHAPTER 5:

THE RIGHT APPROACH

There are lots of fundraising authors and thought leaders who are teaching people a healthier approach to fundraising. Two of my favorites are Jennifer McCrea, who along with her colleague Jeff Walker wrote the book *The Generosity Network*. The other is Nick Fellers from The Suddes Group. Here are just a few of the many solid ideas they taught me. I hope that these concepts will change the way you think about fundraising.

It's not about an exchange. It's about a relationship. Let's face it, asking people for money is not everyone's favorite thing to do. When we change our mindset from asking for money to developing relationships that allow people to give, we allow them to match their passions and dreams to the people we serve; it changes the entire approach. McCrea and Walker talk a lot about a community-based approach to fundraising. The community is made up of the donor, you the fundraiser, and the people you serve. This is very different than the traditional approach to fundraising, where the nonprofit organization is focused primarily on its own needs and agenda.

One of my favorite ideas from McCrea and Walker is the SIM test. This is a test that you give yourself after every donor visit.

1. S—Was I *surprised* by anything?

2. I—Was I *inspired*?

3. M—Was I *moved*?

If you did not answer yes to any of these questions, you were not listening. You were selling or focused on your own agenda.

I took the SIM test on a recent donor visit, and here is what I came up with:

S—I was surprised that the donor had included our organization in his estate plans.

I—I was inspired by his passion for the work we do, giving underprivileged children in third-world countries the tools to live a better life. He'd had a tough childhood himself and wished he'd had someone to help him.

M—I was moved by a powerful, fresh reminder that the work we are doing is making a difference, not just in the children we serve but with our donors. Our donors are part of our mission too.

Nick Fellers and his former partner Tom Suddes talk a lot about impact. In fact, the name of their website is www. forimpact.org. They teach us that most organizations go out to the public with the approach that if we raise enough money, we can have a bigger impact, when in fact it is the opposite. When we lead with the impact, the money (the income) will follow. Tom and Nick profess that our work is about presenting the opportunity for people to invest in our cause to drive impact. Keep in mind that not all of your donors want to do more. I like to use the theory of thirds. Generally, one third of our donor base will give sporadically or lapse eventually. One third will give about the same, perhaps a little more if cultivated properly, and the other third will be open to doing more. This last third are the ones most committed to investing in our work and driving impact. They are the donors who deserve most of our personal attention. We are a bridge, connecting their passions and interests with the needs of those we serve. With that mindset, there is no way we can fail. We are simply creating the opportunity for those donors to do what they need to do.

It's Not About You

A book that had a big influence on me as a young professional was the classic *The 7 Habits of Highly Effective People* by Stephen Covey. It still holds up after all these years. I am continually reminded of a story Stephen told in the book. Here is how I remember the story.

A man was on a train, enjoying his book, when the train pulled up to a station and a father and his children got on the train. The kids started acting up, running around and making noise. The man started to get annoyed and thought to himself, "What is wrong with these kids, and what is wrong with the father that he does not control them?" The man was offended that the father was ruining his quiet train ride. The man was becoming increasingly outraged when the father approached the man and said, "I am sorry; we just came from the hospital. The kids lost their mom today." Ugh. The man felt so ashamed and selfish that he had made it all about him.

I admit I used to take offense to people in that same way. One day at my local supermarket, I approached a cashier who had such a sour look on her face. She did not say hello and appeared annoyed that I was there. My first reaction was to take offense and think to myself, "How dare she not treat me with a courteous smile?" Then I remembered the Covey story and thought to myself, "Who knows what this woman is going through in her personal life?" I told myself, "Be compassionate; don't look for an excuse to be offended." My friend Karen likes to say, "Don't look for a place to park your resentment."

The next time you call a donor and they are short with you, or the next time a donor does not show up for an appointment, remind yourself that it's not about you. It's easy to take that personally, but people are so busy and are under so much pressure to do more with less these days. A great mantra to repeat to yourself is, "It's not about me; it's not about me." That being said, take some time to figure out what it *is* about. Have you spent enough time building trust with the donor? Have you qualified him or her properly? Have you given the donor direct access to your programs to show the impact that giving is having on the people you serve?

Handling Rejection

To approach donors in an authentic and personal way, we have to develop a healthy attitude around rejection. If we go into a donor visit or conversation worried that the donor is going to tell us no, we are never going to connect with that donor because we will be so focused on our own agenda. This is the part of our business that no one likes to talk about, but the fear of rejection has affected all of us at some time or another. We have all heard the stories of wildly successful people who were rejected many times before they were given a chance. Here are a few of my favorites:

- Walt Disney was fired from the *Kansas City Star* newspaper because he "lacked imagination and had no good ideas."

- Oprah Winfrey was fired from one of her first jobs as an evening news reporter because she "couldn't separate her emotions from the news stories."

- Writer Stephen King's first book, *Carrie*, was rejected thirty times. King decided to toss the book, which his wife then went through the trash to rescue and convinced him to resubmit.

- Theodor Seuss Geisel, better known as Dr. Seuss, was rejected by twenty-seven publishers before someone published his first book. By the way, check out *Green Eggs and Ham*. One of my favorite sales books. Yes, sales book. In the book, Sam-I-Am pesters the unnamed character into eating green eggs and ham. He persists until the character eats the green eggs and ham and then thanks Sam-I-Am. I love that—he thanked Sam-I-Am for being so persistent. See the lesson in that?

Rejection is part of life, and it's part of our work as fundraisers. Contractors must work in 100-degree heat, some lawyers must defend guilty people, and morticians must deal with dead bodies. All professions have aspects of the job that aren't fun. Dealing with rejection is one of ours.

There are plenty of people who hear "no" in their jobs all day long. Think of a server at a restaurant. When she asks you if you would like dessert and you say no, she doesn't storm off in a huff or take it personally. She is completely indifferent to your decline of her offer. When I rent a car, the rental agent starts offering all the upgrades—GPS, satellite radio, and extra insurance. All the while I am saying no, and he is not phased one bit. He just keeps on typing away. Anytime I find my ego getting in the way of a decline to my offer, I remember those people and brush it off. It's not easy; it takes practice like anything else.

One of my favorite books is *The Fifth Agreement* by Don Miguel Ruiz. It's an easy read and packed with practical ideas. One of his agreements is "Don't Take Anything Personally." Ruiz teaches us that when we take things personally, we are being selfish by thinking that everything is about us. It's hardly ever about us. Our donors are getting barraged with requests for donations all the time. How selfish is it of us to expect that everyone we approach is going to be open to our offering?

Here are some productive ways to deal with rejection:

- I keep a folder of note cards and e-mails from happy clients and donors who took the time to tell me how grateful they were to work with me. I'll read them on days when I am feeling like no one wants what I am offering.

- There is always going to be a percentage of people who like us, another percentage of people who are indifferent toward us, and another percentage of people who don't like us at all. This is true for everyone. So, if someone rejects you, remind yourself that they are either in the category of indifference or of those who just don't like you, and move on.

- NEXT—I had a colleague many years ago who used that simple and powerful word anytime she was met with rejection. When someone hung up on her, rejected her proposal, or treated her unfairly, she would just yell out "NEXT." We need to let it go and move on as quickly as possible, because there is always someone out there who needs our help.

- Count your noes. If you are not hearing "no" on a consistent basis, then you are not asking enough. You can set a goal for how many noes you hear a week. It's a fun way to change the way you think about the word "no." Every no is closer to a yes. My friend Mary Valle, a salesperson, is a master at dialing and smiling. We worked together a few years back. One day I asked her how her day was, and she responded with, "Well, I got a lot of noes out of the way." Wow, I love that. Mary knows that we are all going to hear "no" and that it's just part of the process.

There are still times, I must admit, when rejection bothers me. Shaking it off quickly takes practice. If you have ever trained a dog, you know that a lot of the training is getting them to break the habit of responding in a nonproductive way. If your dog freaks out every time it sees another dog on your walk, the trainers will tell you to help the dog snap out of it with a command and a treat. With my dog, we use the command "Leave it." I am trying to get him to leave it alone and move on. So too with rejection. When we feel our egos getting in the way and we start getting all worked up, we can shout out a command to ourselves to leave it, move on, let it go, next. And grab yourself a cookie while you are at it.

In my sales days, I had a great mantra I used all the time: "Don't sell, help." When I would approach prospects, some of the more forward prospects would say, "What do you want to sell me?" My reply was always, "I am not here to sell you anything. I am here to see if you need and want my help." That approach did several things. It showed people that I truly cared about their needs and that I was not looking to sell them something they did not need just to make a commission. And it helped me deal with rejection when someone said no. They simply did not need or want my help. I have adapted this mindset to fundraising. "Don't solicit; help." Help donors accomplish what they want through their giving. Help the people we serve live healthier, more productive, and more fulfilled lives.

IF YOU REMEMBER NOTHING ELSE:

✓ Take the SIM test after every donor visit.

✓ When we take things personally, we are making things about us. That's selfish. It's not about us.

✓ Keep moving past the rejection, and Go See People.

CHAPTER 6:

ABUNDANCE MENTALITY

"Abundance is not something we acquire. It's something we tune into."

– Wayne Dyer

So much of daily life is filled with negativity. Turn on the news and you'll find lots of stories about poverty and people suffering. The public tends to focus on what's wrong with our government, people, and their own lives. It's human nature. There are roughly 75,000 domestic flights in the U.S. every day. The news never talks about all the flights that take off and land successfully, only the few that don't. By no means am I dismissing or even minimizing the hardship and suffering that people go through. There is too much of that. That is one of the reasons we do the work we do—to do what we can to make a difference. What I am saying is that to be most effective at helping those people, we need to understand that there are plenty of charitable people with money; it's our job to find those folks. Per *Fortune* magazine, the United States holds 41.6 percent of the world's wealth. The next wealthiest nation is China, with just 10.5 percent of the world's wealth.[4] When you look from that perspective, you can't help but feel hopeful and optimistic about the potential for growing your fundraising program.

Penelope Burke from Cygnus Applied Research found that 52 percent of the donors they surveyed said they would or probably would make a larger gift when they renewed. To clarify, the inclination to increase was based on the charity taking a donor-centered approach. Check out Penelope Burke's book *Donor-Centered Fundraising* at http://cygresearch.com/.

My personal experience as a donor is that most non-profits don't ask often enough—or at all—to increase our giving. I have many personal stories of nonprofits that I have been very involved in—I've even served on their boards—where I sat back waiting for someone to ask me to increase my giving, but no one ever did. I live and breathe fundraising, and it's an important part of my value system, so I may not be in the majority, but there are enough other people like me out there and in your donor file who I am sure would give more if asked in the right way, at the right time, by someone they trust (you).

Here are some ways to tune into the abundance within you:

1. Are you a glass half-full or half-empty person? If you tend to be more pessimistic, you can develop a more

---

4. http://fortune.com/2015/09/30/america-wealth-inequality/

optimistic outlook. It's about retraining your brain to think differently. Expect to succeed. Expect to get what you need. Check out Martin Seligman's book *Learned Optimism*.

2. Anytime you are feeling discouraged, remind yourself that we live in the wealthiest country in the world.

3. Watch whom you are hanging out with. Negative people will try to suck you into their vortex. My friend Bruce likes to say, "Don't get any of that negative goo on me." Love that. If your direct report is negative, do your best to tolerate them, or maybe consider working elsewhere. Talk about abundance, there are 1.4 million 501(c)(3)s in the U.S.

4. Increase your personal donations. I was working with this wonderful donor who told me his personal story about why he is so charitable. He told me that a few years earlier he was in between careers. His wife insisted that they cut back on their donations until their cash flow rose back to normal. He told his wife that was the very reason that they should do the opposite and give more. He felt called by his faith to keep giving it away; that by doing so, God or the universe would provide. I call it karma. I found that the more I try to hold onto something, the more likely it is to hold me hostage.

5. Go see people. Pick up the phone more often. Get out and increase the number of people you connect with every week. This activity is something you have complete control over. The more calls you make, the more people you'll connect with, the more relationships you

will build, and the more money you will raise. Nothing to it, right?

There is a wonderful acronym learned from Sandler Sales Training when I was a young salesperson. Anytime a donor rushes me off the phone or rejects my offer, before I make my next call, I repeat these words:

SW4

Some Will

Some Won't

So What

Someone's Waiting

 IF YOU REMEMBER NOTHING ELSE:

✓ We live in the wealthiest country in the world.

✓ Many donors would donate more if asked.

✓ SW4.

CHAPTER 7:

GIVE AND GET

"You can have everything in life you want, if you will just help other people get what they want."
– Zig Ziglar

Ralph Waldo Emerson wrote a powerful essay called "Compensation." Emerson wrote that the level at which people are compensated is in direct correlation to how much they have contributed. This is a great code to live by and an important one to teach to our children. It's so easy to get caught up in the pressure of performing and getting results that it's easy to forget to help others get what they want.

Start each morning with these simple questions: How can I be of service to people today? How can I help others get what they want? How can I help my donors get what they want? Do I really understand what they want? Have I asked my donors what they want to accomplish through their giving?

There is a wonderful book by Bob Burg and John David Mann titled *The Go-Giver*. We have all heard the term *go-getter*—"She is a real go-getter." It's great to be a go-getter. That's how we bring in the gifts. At the same time, we need to be a go-giver, looking daily for ways to help others get what they want, giving of our time, our resources, and our talent.

I was speaking with a donor who spent most of our time talking about competing charities that he supported at a higher level than the organization I was calling on behalf of. My initial reaction was that he would never be open to a conversation with me about doing more, due to the fact that he was doing so much with these similar organizations. I decided to drop my agenda completely and to just ask questions and listen. I asked him what was important to him in deciding which organizations to support. I asked him why he supported our organization at one level and the others at another level. My reason for asking the questions was not to get what I wanted, but to help him get what he wanted first. I was asking and listening simply to understand and to let him think about, maybe for the first time in a while, why he was so charitable. At the end of the call, he thanked me for listening. He told me he was touched by the conversation and said he wanted to learn more about the work my organization does. He agreed to visit with me. Sometimes we must let go of our agenda and help others with theirs. I would even say that, most times, we are better off doing that.

My friend Florence is a major gifts officer for a community hospital. Florence is a master at helping other people get what they want. Florence will often go above and beyond what is expected of her and will ask donors how she can help them in areas that have nothing to do with their giving. If she is working with a donor who is looking to start or grow a business, Florence will ask the donor whom she can introduce him or her to that might help them with the business or be a potential client. She'll introduce donors to other people in her life who can help them get what they want.

Can You Help Me?

While we want to make helping others a priority, there are times when it's okay to ask others to help us. One of the most powerful questions we can ask someone is "Can you help me?" Most people (especially in fundraising) are cordial and willing to help us if we only ask. Think of all the clichés you have heard over the years: You don't get if you don't ask; Ask and ye shall receive. There is a reason they are clichés: because they are true! There is a wonderful quote attributed to Mark Amend: "Be strong enough to stand alone, smart enough to know when you need help, and brave enough to ask for it."

So why don't we ask for help? Perhaps we are afraid that we are imposing on people. Maybe we think it's a sign of weakness. It does not mean you are weak. Whatever the reason, it only serves to make getting what you want in life more challenging. If someone offers to help, take that person up on it. When we decline someone's offer to help, we are not only rejecting the offer, but we are rejecting him or her as a person as well. People get a lot of satisfaction out of helping people, especially in our business. So don't deny them that satisfaction.

This reminds me of the simple act of taking compliments. Many people are so uncomfortable when taking a compliment. They reply with a self-deprecating comment. If someone says, "You look great," you might reply with, "Please, I have gained so much weight." What you don't realize is that you are rejecting the other person. That individual took the time and perhaps the risk to let you know how he or she felt about you, and you shut that person down by disagreeing. Take the compliment. You don't have to reply with a "so do you." That often seems disingenuous. You can say something like, "Wow, you are so nice to notice. You always know what to say to make people feel good. Thank you."

I recently heard an interview with stand-up comic, actor, and producer Louis C.K. He had an idea for a show he was producing and self-funding. He was not going to try to sell the show to networks, but decided he would charge people to download episodes of the show online, a pretty novel idea at the time of this writing. Louis wanted well-known actors to star in the show, but he had no money or guarantee of money to pay them until people started buying the episodes. Louis approached people like Alan Alda, Steve Buscemi, Jessica Lange, and Edie Falco. Despite no guarantee of getting paid, they all said yes. He even "cold called" Paul Simon and asked him to write the theme song for the show, again with no guarantee of payment, and Simon said yes. Louis called it the "Audacity of the Ask." He had the audacity to ask these very talented and well-paid people to do the project. He had a strong belief in what he was doing, he spoke with passion, and he put it out there. He had the audacity to ask, and people responded.

In her TED Talk "The Art of Asking," musician and performer Amanda Palmer spoke about her "career" and how she made an art of asking people to help her. She is a musician. She defines her music as a cross between punk and cabaret. The music industry has been completely transformed over the last decade. In the digital age of streaming music, musicians, even very popular ones, make little of their income selling their music. Rejected by the major record labels, she decided to give her music away for free and ask for help, relying on the innate kindness of people to reciprocate. Amanda used social media to connect with people to ask them for a place to sleep, a meal, and money for her new album. Through crowdfunding, she raised $1.2 million from 25,000 people. She believes the question is not "how do we make people pay for music?" but "how do we *let* people pay for music?" She did not make people pay for her music; she asked them. Through the very act of asking people, Palmer states she connected with them, and when you connect with them, people want to help you. Amanda ends her talk with this powerful phrase: "Ask without shame." You can see her TED Talk on YouTube. If we don't ask, people don't have the opportunity to give. Or, as Amanda would say, it's not about getting people to donate money, it's about giving them the opportunity to donate and make a difference.[5]

5. https://www.youtube.com/watch?v=xMj_P_6H69g

Go See People

When I started my training and consulting business, I approached several people in fundraising and asked them for their help. I asked each of them if they could introduce me to three fundraisers they knew who would be open to a conversation with me about ways to take their programs to the next level. The response was more than I could imagine. I was so touched by the response of people and their willingness to help me. It proved to me that we can get so much in life if we just ask.

My sales trainer Harry told me a story that was told to him by a man named David Sandler. It's the birdcage story, and it has stayed with me all these years and remains one of my favorite reminders on the power of asking for help.

Imagine you were to buy a birdcage, one of those well-designed ones with multiple levels, maybe made from bamboo. Now, let's say you were to put the cage in an area where a lot of people would see it. No bird, just the cage. Every time someone walked by, you would yell out, "Hey, check out this birdcage!" People would certainly ask, "Where is the bird?" You might reply with several answers, "I am saving up for one of those really exotic birds" or "I am looking to rescue a bird." If you continued this for several months, every chance you got showing people the cage, don't you think at some point you would show up and someone would have put a bird in the cage for you?

People are genuinely good people and want to help others. I see it all the time in life. I was looking for cheap office space when I started my business. At a dinner party one night, I put it out there to the group, and my neighbor Harry said, "We have a salesman who just retired. You are welcome to it, just tell me how much you want to pay."

I was looking for an iPad recently. My friend Russ is an Apple "junkie"; he gets all the latest Apple gadgets when they come out. I called him to ask for advice on which iPad would be best for my needs. Russ offered up one of his barely used iPads for free. I insisted on paying him, but it was significantly less than a new one. You must have examples of your own. So many times, we just need to "put it out there," and people will provide. Call it the law of attraction or the power of intention. No matter what it is you need, chances are there's someone out there willing to help you if only you'll ask.

 IF YOU REMEMBER NOTHING ELSE:

✓ Be a go-giver. Help others get what they want first.

✓ Put your birdcage out there.

✓ Ask without shame.

CHAPTER 8:

CHOICE MANAGEMENT

You know those times when everything hits you at once and you feel like you cannot possibly take anything else on? The thought of being proactive with donor calls and visits seems impossible. A few months ago, I was so busy with work and travel. I had so much going on and I was getting so stressed out over how I was going to get it all done. It seemed like every minute of my week and weekends were filled with something to do.

I was enjoying my morning snack when I felt my tooth crack. In that moment, nothing was more important than getting in to see my dentist, Dr. Robert, to get that tooth fixed. It's funny how our priorities can change at a moment's notice. I called him immediately, got his wife on the phone, and said, "*I don't care what it costs, I really need to see Robert ASAP!*" I cancelled everything I had for that afternoon, and Robert did his magic. I was willing to pay any price to get that tooth fixed.

Driving home that afternoon with half of my face still numb, it hit me that what we so often think is important and urgent will quickly take a backseat to something more urgent. I realized in that moment that I need to make prospect and donor outreach as important as a broken tooth. No excuses, no other options, I must make donor calls a part of my everyday activity, no matter what it takes. And so should you. We need to get past this notion that we don't have time to go see people. I will admit that we are all stretched beyond capacity. Many of us are doing work that we were not hired to do. At the same time, we need to stop convincing ourselves and others that we are too busy to see donors. I truly believe a lot of it comes down to how we think about our daily lives and the work we do. When I get busy, it's easy to tell myself how overwhelmed I am. I stress out over how much I must do, and panic sets in. When I tell myself that everything is under control, that I make great use of my time, and that I am productive, I am more relaxed and I get more accomplished. It's using a bit of the power of positive thinking approach. It works; give it a try.

There are some great books about time management. My two personal favorites are *The ONE Thing* by Gary W. Keller and Jay Papasan, and *Getting Things Done* by David Allen. They are worth reading. (And don't tell me you don't have time to read them!) What I took away from these books and others was that it's all about the choices we make. Maybe it's something in our genetics or maybe we have been raised to feel that if we don't do everything, if we let some things go, we are not being effective. I have struggled with this for years. As a business owner and someone who loves inventing new things, I get very excited by all that is possible. I want to do everything. It's taken me a long time to realize I cannot do everything. I had to give up the things that seemed like great ideas but were not going to grow my business or have a major impact on my clients' success. The great management consultant Peter Drucker once said, "Efficiency is doing things right; effectiveness is doing the right things." I would add to that by saying we need to do the right things right.

Our time is limited; we only have so much of it each day. Our choices, however, are limitless. We need to look at the choices we make each day and ask ourselves throughout the day, "Is this the behavior that I should be doing right now?" As Keller and Papasan point out in *The ONE Thing*, not everything is of equal importance. They suggest we focus on the one thing that matters. That's a little too specific for me, so I focus on the three things each day that matter most.

In *Getting Things Done*, Allen teaches us that we need to capture everything that needs to get done today, this week, this month, this year, and forever, and put them into a logical system outside of our heads and off our minds. Here are two simple examples of this concept in action.

Each morning when I start my day, I write down the three most important things I need to do that day. This frees up my mind to do the best I can do and, most importantly, be present with people. How can we be present with people when our mind is racing with all the things we must do that day?

I keep a notepad and pen at my nightstand so, if in the middle of the night I remember something I forgot to do that day, I can write it down and then I can let it go, to free my mind for a good night's sleep.

Exercise: Write down the three most important things you must do today. Do that every day.

Donor Time

Do you know when your donor time is? Those are the hours of the day that are ideal to speak and meet with your donors. Mine are 10:30 AM to 6:00 PM. My goal on a daily basis is to fill donor time with as many donor conversations as possible, and do all my other tasks before and after that time. If a donor e-mails with something not time-sensitive, I'll save it for that evening or the next morning. If a report is due, I'll work on it before or after donor time. Does that work all the time? No, but I am aware of it all the time. If it's between the hours of 10:30 and 6:00 and I am not speaking with donors, I remind myself that it's donor time, and ask if this task/project can wait. It's about being conscious of how we are spending our time.

The Pareto principle was developed by Vilfredo Pareto. Pareto lived in the late 1800s and early 1900s, when life was much simpler and society moved at a much slower pace. He was way ahead of his time when he discovered that we get 80 percent of our results from 20 percent of our behavior. So, what is the 20 percent that's getting you 80 percent of your results? I understand you have people to answer to and you are expected to do many other things beside seeing donors, but there must be things you are doing that you can delay or stop doing. What can wait? Can you outsource some of the activities that keep you from going to see people? Look at your tasks for the day, and then look to see if someone in your office or a volunteer can do the work. A quick word about volunteers: Please don't be afraid to let volunteers help you. You have plenty out there who want to help. Yes, you need to set parameters and expectations, but the time you invest in doing that and training them will come back many times over with the work your volunteers will do.

Exercise: Take out that legal pad again, and on each line write down, in thirty-minute increments, the hours you will work that day. If you start your day at 8:00 AM, start with 8:00, then 8:30, and so on, up to the time you finish your day. Now, throughout the day, record what you do every half hour. Try this for a couple of days. Then look at your list and determine how much of that time you spent with donors. In my old sales days, they used to say that the average salesperson spent less than 20 percent of his or her day with prospects or customers. Your goal, on a daily basis, should be to increase the time you spend with donors. Stay on a never-ending quest to increase your donor time.

I started using a free online timer to track my activity. When I sit down to make donor calls, I start the clock and stop it when I am finished. This has helped me dramatically increase the time I spend on donor calls. Why? Because I am acutely aware of how I am spending my time through-out the day. When we are very conscious of where we are spending our time each day, then we can start to adjust our behavior. Otherwise, it's easy to finish the week only to discover you have not spent anytime cultivating donor relationships.

I was working with a client recently who kept telling me that she was not making her donor calls. She had just gotten a promotion that came with additional responsibilities, and she was just too busy. I asked her if she could spend just thirty minutes per day making calls. She replied, "I can do anything for thirty minutes a day." It's much less daunting when you break it into little chunks of time. Set your phone timer or use an app, set aside thirty minutes (or even fifteen) per day, and make those calls. Like pushing a stalled car, most of the effort is getting started, then momentum kicks in. Newton said a long time ago that things in motion stay in motion. Once you start, you are more likely to keep going, well beyond the fifteen or thirty minutes.

We all have time to see people. It's about making the right choices and having goals around the number of people you will see each month. For some it might just be two or three people. That's okay; the point is you have a number to work toward.

✑ IF YOU REMEMBER NOTHING ELSE:

✓ What's your 20 percent that is getting you 80 percent of your results?

✓ What hours of your day are donor time?

✓ Use an online timer like www.toggl.com.

CHAPTER 9:

BE THE ETERNAL STUDENT

"Everyone is my teacher. Some I seek. Some I subconsciously attract. Often I learn simply by observing others. Some may be completely unaware that I'm learning from them, yet I bow deeply in gratitude."

– Eric Allen

Being the eternal student is all about seeing everything in life as a lesson, good and bad. They say we learn more from the struggles than the slam dunks. Think about your experiences over the last several years. Which experience taught you the most? Even in the darkest hours, there is a lesson. When my sister Marie was diagnosed with an inoperable brain tumor, when there was nothing anyone could do other than pray, I kept looking for a teaching moment. I asked myself, "What can I learn from this? What can Marie teach me? Is there anything positive that can come out of this?" I did learn so much. Marie taught me that no matter how bleak things look, don't give up faith or hope. She told me, "I won't give up until the miracle appears." She taught me that in life and at the end of it, the only things that matter are relationships and the impact we have on others. I learned that not everything in life works out, and we need to be happy no matter what is going on in our lives. Happiness is something we decide ahead of time. God does not always answer our prayers, at least not the way we hope. Look for the lesson.

I see every donor as a teacher. Before you go into that donor visit, ask yourself, "What can this donor teach me?" This is easy to do with older donors. People who are approaching the ends of their lives are often our best teachers. Bronnie Ware is an Australian nurse who spent several years working in palliative care, caring for patients in the last twelve weeks of their lives. She recorded their dying epiphanies in a blog called *Inspiration and Chai*, which gathered so much attention that she put her observations into a book called *The Top Five Regrets of the Dying*. Here are those top five regrets:

1. I wish I'd had the courage to live a life true to myself, not the life others expected of me.

2. I wish I hadn't worked so hard.

3. I wish I'd had the courage to express my feelings.

4. I wish I had stayed in touch with my friends.

5. I wish that I had let myself be happier.

Don't wait, seize the moment.

If you are not already working towards an advanced degree, pretend you are. Decide to spend thirty to sixty minutes a day studying your craft. You can pick topics from this book (or others) and treat each one like a separate course. Take thirty days per topic to learn everything you can about it. For example, in Month 1 you can study everything you can about listening. In Month 2, learn how to ask better questions, and so on.

Study books. I am talking about business, fundraising, and self-development books here. Don't just read them: study them. I start by reading the cover and learning about the author. What's their background, what's their agenda? Then I go to the table of contents and look at all the sections and chapters, getting an understanding of how the book is structured. I will highlight the chapters in the table of contents that seem most helpful. As I read the book, I'll take notes with pen and paper, pulling out the ideas I can use. After finishing the book for the first time, I'll go through and reread the sections that were most relevant to me. If the book is helpful, I'll download the audio version and keep listening to it repeatedly until the ideas are ingrained in my brain and I take action on them.

Quick Tip

Research has shown that the best way to learn is to take what you are reading and studying and explain it to someone else. You have not learned something unless you can teach it to someone else. If you are teaching or training your team, or even your child, make sure you ask them to repeat back to you what they learned in their own words. Telling is not teaching.

Exercise: Keep a "lessons learned" journal. On a weekly or monthly basis, write down the lessons you learned that month. Each time you do that, review the lessons from the past to remind yourself not to repeat them. Here is an example from my journal.

"I thought I was prepared for the meeting with the prospect. Her expectation of the meeting turned out to be very different from mine. Make no assumptions. Ask the prospect what they are specifically hoping to accomplish in the meeting ahead of time."

 IF YOU REMEMBER NOTHING ELSE:

✓ We learn more from the setbacks than the successes.

✓ Look for the lesson in everyone and every experience.

✓ "The wise learn from adversity; the foolish repeat it." – Proverb

CHAPTER 10:
SMILE

Smile, though your heart is aching
Smile, even though it's breaking
When there are clouds in the sky
you'll get by
If you smile through your fear and sorrow
Smile and maybe tomorrow
You'll see the sun come shining through
for you
             – "Smile," Lyrics by John Turner and
    Geoffrey Parsons, Music by Charlie Chaplin

A chapter on smiling, really? Yes, really. As I have mentioned, so much of growing and increasing our success comes from improving the little things that we take for granted. When I started getting serious about making live presentations and producing videos, I decided to hire a video coach. We did a lot of work on film. The big thing that my coach taught me was to smile while I was talking. Early video feedback showed that I hardly smiled at all. When I did smile, it was in between sentences and it looked phony. It was difficult at first, but after a lot of practice and sore cheeks, I have learned to smile while I speak, both in front of live audiences and on video. I constantly have to remind myself to do it, but I am getting better. I became very aware of watching great presenters who smile while they speak. One of my favorite examples of this is CNN anchor Robin Meade. She has this beautiful smile that she maintains while she is speaking (unless she is doing a sad story).

Smiles draw people in. I love to do experiments on smiling when I am out in public. I'll make eye contact with complete strangers and give them a smile. I count how many people respond with a smile. The vast majority do, and it makes them feel better. Smiles are contagious!

There is something physiological about smiling as well. Self-development guru Tony Robbins talks about standing up, lifting your head high, and smiling. He says while we are in that physical state, it's impossible to feel negative or sad. It's a great exercise to do when you are having a tough day. It's also a great habit to develop when you are making your donor calls.

Quick Tip

Stand up and smile while you are leaving a voicemail or speaking to a donor on the phone. People can feel the smile through the phone. I find that it gives me a more pleasant tone.

Exercise: Get your phone out and video yourself doing a mini presentation. Are you smiling? Try it again. Exaggerate your smile so it feels unnatural at first and watch the playback. It's an eye (and mouth) opening experience. If your cheeks don't hurt after doing this, you're not smiling enough.

✍ IF YOU REMEMBER NOTHING ELSE:

✓ Smile even when you don't feel like it; it will make you feel better.

✓ Next time you walk down a busy street, take note of how many people smile. Be the one who smiles the brightest.

CHAPTER 11:
GRATITUDE

Gratitude is a powerful process for shifting your energy and bringing more of what you want into your life. As Rhonda Byrnes wrote in her book *The Secret,* "Be grateful for what you already have and you will attract more good things."

Rhonda speaks a lot about gratitude. I read something in her book that stuck with me all these years, and that's to be grateful for every little thing in my life. As you walk down the street, be grateful for the blue sky. Be grateful that you can walk. She also taught me to look for something to be grateful for in the things that seem to be a nuisance. When you are driving down the road and come to a standstill in traffic because road crews are working on the road, don't get upset. Be grateful for those people who keep the roads safe. When you are sitting outside relaxing and a landscaper is disrupting your peace and quiet with the sound of his mower, be grateful he is there to keep your neighborhood looking clean and beautiful.

All this might sound like new-age nonsense to some, but it works. Every time I feel a negative emotion coming on, I stop and look for things I am grateful for in the moment.

Jack Canfield said it so well in his blog post "6 Daily Habits of Gratitude That Will Attract More Abundance and Joy into Your Life":

> "Daily habits of gratitude and appreciation are one of the highest emotional states you can experience. When you cultivate gratitude, you're able to feel true joy and contentment, no matter what you have or don't have in your life. The Law of Attraction states that like attracts like, when you're grateful for what you already have, you will naturally attract more for which you can be grateful".

Standing in Gratitude

When you are in a bad mood or frustrated, quickly shift your thoughts to what you are grateful for. It's a simple but powerful shift that can turn your bad mood into joy.

When you are struggling to grow your major gifts program and no one seems to want to give, be thankful for the donors you do have and the level at which they give. Keep reminding yourself of how much you and your organization have. You'll be surprised at how it changes your way of being with donors too! But don't get too comfortable—our job is to grow the program.

Years ago, my sales trainer Harry told me a story he called the Doberman story. He explained that Doberman Pinschers (as well as most dogs) can sense when a human is afraid of them. Harry explained that people (donors) can sense when we are nervous, anxious, or maybe feeling desperate, like we are desperate for the money. Yes, there are times when we all feel anxious or preoccupied with our own feelings. Donors can sense when we are anxious or feeling pressured to get the gift. That pressure transfers to the donor and makes them uneasy. No one likes to be pressured into anything. When we stand (or sit) in gratitude, grateful for just the opportunity to visit with the donor, grateful for all they have already done, we put the donor at ease. The more donors are at ease, the faster we build trust and the more likely they are to want to spend more time with us. The key is to adjust your thinking and mindset to one of abundance, joy, and gratitude.

Quick Tip

Every morning when you awake, as you get out of bed, when your one foot touches the floor, say "thank"; when the other foot touches the floor, say "you." Thank you, thank you for this gift of another day.

IF YOU REMEMBER NOTHING ELSE:

✓ Find the joy and blessings in all the minor annoyances of life.

✓ Donors can sense your anxiety. Stay in the moment; stay in gratitude.

> *"Be thankful for what you have; you'll end up having more. If you concentrate on what you don't have, you will never, ever have enough."*
> *– Oprah Winfrey*

SECTION II:

BEHAVIOR

"Ideation without execution is delusion."
– Robin Sharma

Good ideas are a dime a dozen. Over the years, I have had so many conversations around developing new programs, businesses, offerings, events, and more. Most of them never saw the light of day. Sure, it's important to continually look for better ways to do something. My experience is that many people get stuck in executing those ideas. There are several reasons for this. Some are perfectionists and need to have everything perfectly in place before starting. Newsflash: It's never going to be the ideal time to do anything. If in your heart you feel it's the right thing to do, then execute. There is an old expression from the military: Any action is better than no action. Or another favorite of mine, sometimes 80 percent is good enough. If the task at hand or decision involves a lot of investment in time and money and has a lot of risk associated with it, 80 percent is probably not enough, but for all those other times when the risk is low, just pull the trigger and figure out the other 20 percent as you go along. Most times, the outcome is rarely what you think it is going to be anyway.

Many times, I see people lack clarity around what's most important to them and the people involved with the idea. Good execution includes clarity, proper planning, goal setting, and tracking behavior and results.

CHAPTER 12:
GOAL SETTING

Written goals are one of those things that everyone knows they should have, but very few actually do have. The percentage of people who track their goals on a consistent basis is even smaller. I am all about keeping goals simple. In fact, some research has shown that if you have more than three goals, you have too many and you are far less likely to achieve any of them. Keep in mind there is a difference between goals, objectives, and tasks. Goals are overriding principles. Objectives are steps we take to meet those goals, and tasks are the day-to-day behaviors needed for everything else to happen.

Most people set SMART goals. You are probably familiar with the SMART acronym. It stands for Specific, Measurable, Attainable, Relevant, and Time-bound. It's a great way to test your goals to make sure they are effective. I do have an issue with the attainable part. Why? Because we tend to set our goals too low. We play it safe.

I like to set three levels for each of my goals.

1. Attainable. These I set when I am accountable to other people (board members, leadership, donors).

2. BHAGs. Jim Collins coined this acronym, which stands for Big Hairy Audacious Goals, in his book *Good to Great*. These are goals I only share with my inner circle. I take my SMART goals and jack them up. Consistently, each year, I finish somewhere between my SMART goals and my BHAGs. The BHAGs force us to think differently. Albert Einstein taught us to solve problems with new ways of thinking.

3. Open space. This is a third type of goal that I have recently discovered from author and leadership consultant Robert Cooper, who calls them open-space goals. In his book *Get Out of Your Own Way,* Cooper writes, "Open space is where you can move from beyond good and great into something deeper, next, and more. It's where the 'impossible' happens…where you devote yourself to surpassing your own previous best efforts, not by an inch but by a mile."

Let me give you an example of how to turn a SMART goal into an open-space goal. Let's say you are an organization whose mission is to feed the poor. A SMART goal could be to feed ten thousand people a day for the next twelve months. A BHAG goal would be to double or triple the number of people fed in a day. Great goals, right? An open-space goal, however, would be to end poverty completely so that no one would ever have to go a day without missing a meal. The more we stretch our thinking, the more we realize what is possible.

Exercise: What is your open space goal? Think about your mission. What could an open space goal be? Free tuition for all students? Ending world hunger? A world without slavery?

Goal Tracking

Goals are not something you write down, put in your drawer, and never look at again until the end of the year. Your written goals should be a part of your daily focus.

Every Monday morning, before I start my week, I write down my three top goals. I break my goals into three categories: relationships, business, and health. As of this writing, my goals for this year in each of those areas are:

1. *Relationships:* One family event per week. A family event could be a date with my wife, taking my mom to lunch, or spending time with one of my nieces or nephews.

2. *Business:* Fill forty billable hours of client work per week.

3. *Health:* Consume 50 percent less food and drink per week.

The physical act of writing them down and sharing them with my family and friends every week keeps my goals tattooed on my brain so I never forget. That keeps me focused on what's most important.

You should share your goals and ask others to hold you accountable for those goals. I share my goals with my wife and ask her to hold me accountable. When she sees me getting distracted, she asks me what my top three goals are to bring me back on track.

I was in a parking lot recently and on the back of a minivan window was a list that looked like this:

_X_5K

_X_10K

___Half Marathon

___Marathon

Every day that person had her goals staring her in the face. She had clarity on where she was and where she needed to go. She put it out there for everyone to see. The only thing missing was the time frame she would complete the races in, but you get the idea.

✍ IF YOU REMEMBER NOTHING ELSE:

✓ Jack up your goals.

✓ Commit to your top three goals. Write them down every week.

✓ Start thinking bigger and you'll achieve more.

CHAPTER 13:

TRACK RESULTS AND BEHAVIOR

Most people do a good job at tracking results. Dollars in the door, pledges, and intentions are all straightforward. Well, what is the behavior that is needed to obtain those results? That's the area I don't see a lot of people focusing on. After all, the only thing we have complete control over is our behavior. I can control how many times I pick up the phone to call a donor. I can control how many letters and e-mails I send. I can control how many doors I knock on. I can control how many people I introduce myself to at an event. I cannot control whether someone will answer the phone, respond favorably, or agree to a conversation.

My favorite behavior to track is Dials. Dials are the number of times you pick up the phone to call a prospect or donor. The first step is to set a goal for how many dials you would like to make in a given time period, be it daily, weekly, or monthly. Once you have that number, you should know how many dials you have completed at any given time. Let's say you set a goal to make fifty dials per week. That's picking up the phone fifty times every week to connect with a prospect or donor. I don't include hang ups and bad numbers, only valid numbers that can lead to a conversation. It's tracking the one thing you can control: picking up the phone and dialing. When you are tracking those dials properly, you'll know exactly where you are toward your goal of fifty at any given time. If I called you on any given Thursday, you should have that number right on the tip of your tongue.

Quick Tip

Every Friday afternoon, just before you are ready to pack up for the weekend, pick up the phone and make one more call. Call that prospect you meant to call all week. Watch how many times someone answers with a warm greeting. You never know where it might lead. Just make that one more call!

So how many dials do you need to make each week? Depends on your batting average.

Batting Average

If a Major League Baseball player is batting .300, he is doing really well. That means for every ten times up to bat, he will get a hit three times. What's your batting average? How many times do you need to pick up the phone to connect with a donor? How many times do you need to connect with a donor to get a visit, and how many visits do you need to make to get a gift? The best way to figure this out is to start tracking your behavior. Keep track of how many calls you make, how many times you connect with a donor, how many visits you make, and so on. From my own personal experience and speaking with a number of fundraisers over the years, I use a success rate of 20 percent. This number will vary based on a number of factors, such as the type of organization, loyalty of donors, and the fundraising culture of the organization.

Here is how I came up with that percentage: For every ten calls I make, I will connect with two people (20 percent). This may not be right away, but within a week or so of calling. For every five people I connect with, at least one will be open to a conversation or a visit (20 percent). For every five people I visit with, one should be open to a gift (depending on where we are in the relationship and other factors). That's another 20 percent.

Now, let's say I am a planned giving officer. I know my average bequest is $60,000. If you don't know your average bequest, use the national average of $40,000. If my goal is to identify $600,000 in planned gift commitments this year, I can determine the behavior required to do that based on the above formula. It looks something like this:

We have a goal of $600,000 in planned gift commitments. We know that our average bequest is $60,000. That's ten commitments or ten donors saying yes ($60,000 × 10 = $600,000). To get ten donors to say yes, I need to visit with fifty people. To meet with fifty people, I need to connect with 250 people. To connect with 250 donors, I need to make 1,250 calls. That's 104 calls per month, or twenty-six calls per week, or about five calls a day. Surely anyone can make five calls per day.

You can create a simple form and use a tally mark system. Your form may look like this:

Month: October

Dials

~~|||| |||| |||| |||| |||| |||| |||| |||| |||| |||| ||||~~

~~|||| |||| |||| |||| |||| |||| |||| |||| |||| ||||~~

Connects

~~|||| |||| |||| |||| ||||~~

Visits

~~||||~~

Gifts

|

Knowing our batting average helps in several ways. First, it enables us to determine how much activity we need to get the results we want. Second, it keeps us motivated on days when no one seems to be answering the phone or responding to our outreach. There are plenty of times when I have made twenty-five or thirty calls a day without reaching or hearing from anyone. Like clockwork, within a day or two, there are several e-mails or voicemails in my inbox from donors responding. If a donor takes the time to return a call, they are most often engaged enough to be open to a conversation.

The power of dial goals. It was a beautiful August Friday afternoon in Philadelphia, one of those summer days with low humidity and a perfect breeze. I had just left a client's office. It was 11:30. I had no other commitments for the rest of the day and had this great idea to grab my bike and head up to the country to enjoy the afternoon. I looked down in my passenger seat and saw my dial tracker form. My goal for that week was to make fifty dials. I had only made forty dials. I thought for a moment, "No one will know; just knock off early and you'll make it up next week." Then I thought, how can I get paid to tell others to make their dials every week if I am not doing that? So, I pulled into a parking lot, got out my prospect list, and made my ten additional calls. Now I was praying no one would answer the phone so I could get on the bike, but lo and behold, two people did answer. One person told me that they were thinking about going into a campaign the following year and were open to chatting. The other person was a woman I had been pursuing who told me she was so glad I called and was apologetic for not being responsive. One of those calls ultimately developed into a great client. Had I not been fully committed to my fifty dials per week, who knows what I would have missed?

Determine your batting average, make your calls, and Go See People.

Exercise: Here is a great little game to play. At the next social, donor, or cultivation event you attend, set a goal to collect a certain number of business cards from people you don't know. Your goal may be to collect five before the event is over.

Qualify People

As I get older, I get tired of chasing people. As someone who has spent so many years selling, if I was pursuing a prospect, donor, or client and gave up too soon, I considered myself as having failed. There is a fine line between being persistent and wasting time on someone who has no interest in what we are offering. If I connect with someone who has interest, belief, and capacity, I'll be professionally persistent all the way. If I find myself chasing someone though, I know that I am neglecting the people who need my help. So, I have been working hard on qualifying people to see how interested or committed they are. I am not saying we should not give people a second chance, but a third, fourth, or fifth chance? You must decide for yourself if it's worth chasing someone. This approach is especially important if you are a major or planned gift officer working with a qualified pool of 150 donors. You cannot afford to chase a donor who is not interested. Take them off your 150 qualified donors list and replace them with someone else. Watch how people respond to you and give them little tests to gauge their commitment level.

Here is an example to demonstrate what I mean. As a disclaimer—you have to keep several things in mind. The person may be introverted and uncomfortable in certain social situations, or they may be interested but over-whelmed with a personal or work matter.

Scenario—You are at a social or business event. You strike up a conversation with someone you don't know. After a nice conversation, you ask the person for his business card. He has asked very little about what you do, and he doesn't even ask you for your business card. Is he interested? Now, if this is a significant potential donor, client, or prospective employer, I am not suggesting you give up right away, but it is worth making a mental note of the individual's behavior.

The scenario continues. The person did not ask for your card, but you ask him if he is open to a second conversation. He says sure. You tell him you will e-mail him. The next day you e-mail him, and he doesn't respond. Two days later you call. No response. Okay, time to do a reality check. Is this person blowing smoke? Is he worth pursuing? That's the second sign he may not be serious.

You have a third interaction. The person finally gets back to you two weeks later and does not apologize or make any mention of responding so late. He agrees to a phone conversation and either postpones or is fifteen minutes late for the call. Sign number three. Do you keep chasing this person or move on? That's the decision you need to make. Are you wasting not only time but emotional energy that you could be spending with other people who are receptive to your message, mission, cause, outreach, and proposal? NEXT!

As a fundraising consultant and business owner, I have been qualifying prospective clients for a while now, and it has made my life so much more enjoyable. Years ago, before I learned about qualifying people, I was referred to a potential client who seemed to fit my ideal prospect profile. It was a small college that had a basic major and planned giving program, but the board and leadership wanted to ramp it up. I was referred to the director of development. I left an e-mail and voicemail for the prospect and I received no response (Warning #1). I called again and did get him on the phone. He said he was open to a conversation but rushed me off the phone. He asked me to call his admin to set an appointment (Warning #2). I set the appointment with his admin and he cancelled the call one hour before (Warning #3). I e-mailed his admin, per his request, to set another phone appointment. He did show for that call but he was ten minutes late for the call (Warning #4). As the relationship progressed, I was very cautious, and my gut told me that this guy would not be someone I wanted to do business with. Thankfully, I was not awarded the contract. I was a little upset about it for a short time. As God and the universe always seem to provide, I wound up picking up two new clients who were an absolute joy to work with.

It finally occurred to me that I was qualifying potential clients as ideal by the type, size, and maturity of their program. What I failed to realize was that it was not enough. I learned I needed to start doing a better job at qualifying the people in the organization. Are they collaborative? Will they be accountable? Will they do their homework? Are they trainable? Are they responsive? So, I now give prospective clients little tests. Do they respond to my e-mails? Am I always calling them, or do they initiate a call occasionally? I send them a free copy of one of my books. Do they acknowledge the book or never make mention of it?

I give them a little homework. I might ask them to fill out a short survey or read a short article I wrote. If they don't send back the survey or read the article by the time we meet, a red flag goes up that they may not be committed. So, if you are a consultant or salesperson reading this—get better at qualifying people. It's important to keep an abundance mentality. You may do a great job of selling this person, but more often than not, they will quickly become a nightmare client. Move on.

If you are a fundraiser, you also need to qualify people. I took a cue from the movie *Glengarry Glen Ross*. There is a haunting phrase repeated in the movie by Alec Baldwin's character, "ABC—Always Be Closing." I have adapted that to ABQ—Always Be Qualifying.

You cannot dismiss donors. That's not what this is about. Working with donors is different than sales, and we need to handle all relationships thoughtfully. You can, however, qualify donors using these tips to see if they are ready to do more now, down the road, or never.

IF YOU REMEMBER NOTHING ELSE:

✓ Know your batting average and the number of times you need to pick up the phone each day, week, and month.

✓ ABQ—always be qualifying people to determine if they are ready to go to the next level of the relationship or not.

CHAPTER 14:

TEST

"Anything worth doing long term is worth testing short term."

– Bruce Morrow

That's great advice from my friend Bruce Morrow. There is so much information online about pretty much anything you want to learn. Often, people will ask me what works for annual, major, or planned giving outreach. My response is, "This works for other people or organizations, but the only way you are going to know if it works for you is to test it." This is a simple point, but a big one as well. We don't test enough. Or we don't do it in a systematic way. Test as many things as you can. I think of a scientist going to work each day with their lab coat and clipboard. Scientists don't assume anything. They determine what works by experimenting, testing, measuring, and then adjusting until the desired result is achieved. We should do the same with our work. I learned from direct mail experts many years ago that you need to test one component at a time.

Let me show you what I mean.

Voicemails

My favorite things to test are my voicemails. What is the right combination of words, inflection, pace, and tone to deliver more compelling voicemails that encourage donors to call me back? Let's start by breaking down the components of a voicemail:

Length. How long are your voicemails? People have such short attention spans. To measure the length, leave yourself a voicemail. It should ideally be less than sixty seconds. How can you make the message more concise and more compelling?

Content. This contains your call to action. What do you want the donor to do? Call you? E-mail you? Visit? Is that call to action clear? What seems to get the best response?

Tone/Pace. This is how you say it. As important as *what* you say is, it's probably more important *how* you say it. What is your tone? Is it light and comfortable? Is it bubbly? Too bubbly? How about your pace? Is it too slow or too fast? When I started working with older donors on the phone, I had one older donor tell me to slow down because she could not understand what I was saying. That was a big wake-up call for me. I did not even realize that I was speaking so fast. You may consider adjusting your tone and pace for the donor. If you know the donor is older and maybe from a rural area where the pace of life is slower, tone it down and slow it down. If you are speaking with a busy Wall Street executive, you may consider slightly increasing your pace and tone.

What Are You Saying?

You can take the content component and test different messages. When I started making donor calls for one organization a while ago, I quickly found out that I was giving away too much information on the voicemail. My message sounded something like this:

"Hi Mary, this is Joe from ABC Relief Fund. I am calling you to set a time for us to chat on the phone to thank you personally for your generosity over the years, learn about why you give, update you on the impact those gifts are having, and see how we can be better stewards of your donations."

Well, what started happening was that some donors did call me back, and left me voicemails that sounded like this:

"Hi Joe, this is Mary, returning your call. You don't need to thank me. Everything is fine, I trust you folks are using the money wisely. No need to call me back."

Alrighty then. So, it only took two voicemails like that until I realized I had to test a new voicemail message. I was giving them too much information. So, I adjusted the voicemail to sound something like this:

"Hi Mary, this is Joe from ABC Relief Fund. I am calling you to set a time for us to chat on the phone to thank you for your generosity, ask you a few questions, and update you on a new initiative we are rolling out."

That message worked much better. I did not get anyone leaving me messages saying there was no need to chat. I then went to work on my follow-up. I thought about the most effective way to follow up and started testing different approaches, like sending an e-mail follow-up, sending a handwritten note, and sending a postcard.

As always, your results will vary depending on many variables. The point is to keep testing. Determine what is going to produce the best results in your situation, with your constituency and with your unique style.

Here is a partial list of things you can test:

- Voicemails

- E-mails

- Pre-call letters

- Notecards

- An "I have not been able to reach you" survey. Send these to donors whom you cannot connect with. In the survey, ask them the questions you were going to ask them on the phone, and include a return envelope.

- Meeting with donors at their office (or yours) versus their home or a restaurant.

- Bringing someone with you on a donor visit versus going it alone.

- Doing research on your donor before the first visit versus going into the meeting with only his or her giving history.

- Types of questions you ask your donor.

- Telling your story with a computer presentation versus a paper presentation versus just you telling the stories.

- Telling donor stories versus stories of people who benefit from your mission.

See Chapter 22 for more on creating voicemails that inspire donors to call you back.

 IF YOU REMEMBER NOTHING ELSE:

✓ Anything worth doing long-term is worth testing short-term.

✓ Just because something works for someone else, it does not mean it will work for you. You have to test it to find out.

✓ Like the researcher looking for a cure for a disease, stay insatiably curious, continually looking for a better result.

CHAPTER 15:
WRITE IT DOWN

Another great success tool I learned from my friend Bruce is to write things down. Bruce calls it TPOP (Think and Plan on Paper). Once again, this is a habit we all should develop, but one that very few of us do on a consistent basis. I am talking about good old-fashioned paper and pen. There has been so much research on the power of writing things down.

Dustin Wax has researched and written on this topic. Wax writes:

> *When we write something down, research suggests that, as far as our brain is concerned, it's as if we were doing that thing. Writing seems to act as a kind of mini-rehearsal for doing. Visualizing doing something can "trick" the brain into thinking it's actually doing it, and writing something down seems to use enough of the brain to trigger this effect. Again, this leads to greater memorization, the same way that visualizing the performance of*

a new skill can actually improve our skill level. The first thing just about every personal productivity writer in the world tells us is to write everything down. If you're a "writer-downer," you know how important this is, and you know that it works.[6]

Thinking and planning on paper and writing things down can take many shapes. Here are a few ways you can apply this concept:

- Every morning, write down your top three goals. Sometimes I write mine on a piece of scrap paper, then throw it out at the end of the day. As we learned in Dustin Wax's writings, that physical act of writing them down forces me to remember my goals and keeps them at the top of my mind all day. See Chapter 12 for more on goal setting.

- When attending a webinar, conference, or training session, take notes. Even if you never look at those notes again, something will stick.

- Mindstorm. I love this exercise. In Chapter 3: Think Big, I called it brainstorming. You can apply this to any area of your life. You come up with a question you want to answer and write down at least twenty answers (ideas). No ideas are bad. Once you have completed the list, pick three ideas and implement them within sixty days. Here are a few questions to help you think of some of your own:

---

6. http://www.lifehack.org/articles/featured/writing-and-re-membering-why-we-remember-what-we-write.html

- How can I be a better spouse/partner/father/mother?

- How can I lose the weight and get in better shape?

- How can I start that business I always wanted to start?

- How can we double our board giving?

- How can we possibly raise ten times more money than we raised last year?

This is a great exercise to do at your next development or board retreat.

 IF YOU REMEMBER NOTHING ELSE:

✓ If you don't write it down, you're not serious about doing it.

✓ Writing things down increases the stickiness factor.

CHAPTER 16:

THE RULE OF THREES

According to Wikipedia, the Rule or Power of Threes is a writing principle that suggests things are funnier, more memorable, and more impactful when presented in threes.[7] Think of all the stories, characters, and movies in pop culture—The Three Stooges, The Three Musketeers, the Three Little Pigs. In comedy, many jokes are based on three characters. This is yet another simple idea that is easy to incorporate and can be very effective in many areas of your life. Marketing companies do it all the time. There is a psychology around pricing and buying decisions. If you give someone three price options—a low price, a medium price, and a high price—they are more likely to pick the middle one.

You must be careful with this concept. It can come across as manipulative. However, if all three offers are presented for the mutual benefit of your organization

---

7. Wikipedia, s.v. "Rule of Three," retrieved from https://en.wikipedia.org/wiki/Rule_of_three_(writing)

and the donor, it may be a great way to help donors make good decisions. For example, your annual appeal reply card can offer three suggested giving levels: $100, $250, and $500. It's recommended that your giving levels be segmented based on each of your donors' prior giving level. This is not a book about annual giving, but you get the idea. The rule of threes makes life so much simpler!

Here are some practical applications:

Three-point agenda. You should never go into a planned phone call or meeting without an agenda. I love to use the three-point agenda. It gives me clarity around what's most important, it helps me organize my thoughts, and it shows the attendees that there is a purpose and a plan for the meeting. Most people spend too much time in meetings. We should continually evaluate the need for meetings and how to make them more productive. Here is an example of a three-point agenda for a meeting with a board member:

1. Discuss your 2017 fundraising plan.
2. Get your feedback on how to grow our individual gifts' program.
3. See how we can be better stewards of your donations and time.

Top three values. I use this one quite a bit when advising people who are looking for new jobs or careers. My first question is, what are your top three values when it comes to the work that you want to be doing?

Here are my top three values around the work I do:

1. It's important for me to be independent. I have not been an employee or received a W-2 in over thirty years.

2. I need to do work that gives purpose to my life.

3. I need to do work that excites me, work that I love to do.

If you are in a good financial position that allows you to be more discerning with a job, your three values should drive the decision on your new job or new business undertaking. What are your top three values? Write them down. Next time you get an offer for a new job, go back to your values: Does the opportunity fit your core values? If you are single and looking for a partner, you may consider getting very clear on the top three values you admire in another person.

Top three reasons for a donor to meet with you. Your voicemails and e-mails should give donors good reasons why they should meet with you. Give them three reasons. Here are three I use. See if you can come up with more:

1. Thank you personally for your giving.

2. Update you on how you are making a difference with those we serve.

3. See how we can improve how we are serving you and your experience as a donor.

Three Easy Steps. Here is a great one to use when developing marketing and communications materials to promote planned giving. Give the donor three simple steps to follow. The following is an example of marketing planned giving for a fictitious Museum:

You can include ABC Museum as a beneficiary of your retirement plan. Take these three easy steps:

1. Call your retirement plan administrator for a beneficiary form.

2. Designate ABC Museum as a partial or full beneficiary.

3. Let us know so we can celebrate your gift while you are alive.

 IF YOU REMEMBER NOTHING ELSE:

✓ Remember the rule of threes. It will help you organize your thoughts, deliver a memorable message, and stay on point.

CHAPTER 17:
PLANNING

"Give me six hours to chop down a tree and I will spend the first four sharpening the axe."
— Abraham Lincoln

Love that quote from Honest Abe. Though life was much simpler (and much harder) then, President Lincoln knew the benefits of planning. Since that time, many self-development and time-management gurus have shown that just thirty minutes of planning can save you hours of execution. Despite that, the thought of planning seems like such a waste of time and energy. Forget all that planning; let's just do the work, right? I had a history of being in the "let's just get started" camp, rushing through activities and projects only to find later that I either should have done things differently or that I'd spent my time doing the wrong things. That's worth reflecting on. Are you spending your time doing the wrong things? As we discussed in Chapter 8, it's about making the right choices.

While not planning at all is a recipe for disaster, over analysis—as the saying goes—can lead to paralysis. Sometimes 80 percent is good enough. Sometimes, but not always.

My longtime friend Andrei Jablokow says it so well:

The more time you spend planning, refining your plan, and writing it down in simple language, the better your chances of being successful. Writing down your plan creates clarity in your thinking, forces you to focus on what is important, helps commit your ideas to long-term memory, and enables you to communicate your ideas to others who can help you. A written plan reduces distraction on shiny new ideas that may or may not lead to reaching your primary objective sooner. By putting your best plan into action, you can't help but be successful.

Proper planning will

- Help you prioritize what's most important.
- Prepare you for the worst and motivate you to expect the best.
- Reduce stress by getting everything out of your head and down on paper.
- Force you to come up with ideas you never thought of.
- Give you clarity.

Here are some common areas where a little bit of planning goes a long way:

Your ideal week. Plan your week. Write down the three most important things you should be doing this week. You can also write down the things you won't do (a not-to-do list). For example, you may write: I won't get distracted by unimportant e-mails, social media, or office gossip.

Ninety-day plan. My friend Bruce Morrow turned me on to the ninety-day plan. It's brilliant in its simplicity. Take out a blank piece of paper (or create a document in Word or Excel). Using a landscape orientation, divide the sheet into three equal sections. At the top of each section, going from left to right, list the current month, next month, and the next month after that. Now, in each section, write down all the things you want or must do for each month. At the end of each month, fill out a fresh sheet and carry forward the tasks or projects you did not complete that month. The ninety-day plan fits well with David Allen's *Getting Things Done* system (referenced in Chapter 8).

Donor visits. Please don't tell me you go into donor visits without taking some time to determine what you want to learn about the donor and accomplish on the visit. Also, think about what your donor might want to learn and accomplish. Be sure to ask them when you get there.

Development plan. Development plans can be fifty-page documents or simple two to three-page plans. The point is to make sure you have a written one and to track your progress on a weekly basis. Once again, this may be common sense, but not everyone has one and monitors it properly. And make sure planned giving is in there!

Board fundraising plan. What's the plan for your board? What's the total board giving goal this year?

Where in the donor relationship management process is each board member going to participate this year? Will they help with identification, cultivation, solicitation, or stewardship?

Board recruiting plan. What is the plan to add board members or encourage hangers-on to roll off the board?

Marketing plan. All your marketing should start with a written plan. Sounds like common sense, but I am surprised by how many development shops I go into that don't have one. Keep it simple. A one-page marketing plan will often suffice.

Too Much Planning

There is a fine line between planning and over planning. In their book *Fail Fast, Fail Often*, Ryan Babineaux and John Krumboltz tell this great story they learned in the book *Art and Fear* by Bayless and Orland that demonstrates the difference between proper and excessive planning. I retell it in my own words below.

> *The ceramics teacher announced on opening day that he was dividing the class into two groups. All those on the left side of the studio, he said, would be graded solely on the quantity of work they produced, all those on the right solely on the quality. His procedure was simple: on the final day of class, he would bring in his bathroom scales and weigh the work of the quantity group: fifty pounds of pots rated an "A," forty pounds a "B," and so on. Those being graded on quality, however, needed to produce only one pot—albeit a perfect one—to*

get an "A."

Well, come grading, a curious fact emerged: The works of the highest quality were all produced by the group being graded for quantity. It seems that while the quantity group was busily churning out piles of work—and learning from their mistakes—the quality group had sat theorizing about perfection, and in the end had little more to show for their efforts than grandiose theories and a pile of dead clay.

It's only by DOING—and being willing to make mistakes—that we learn and get better!

We are either part of our own plan or someone else's. It's our choice. Choose wisely, my friend.

✍ IF YOU REMEMBER NOTHING ELSE:

✓ Planning now will save time later.

✓ Written plans don't have to be lengthy to be effective.

CHAPTER 18:

CLARITY

"We value integrity; we follow clarity."
– Andy Stanley

What did Martin Luther King, Mahatma Gandhi, Nelson Mandela, and Steve Jobs all have in common? They had clarity. They knew exactly what their purpose was, what needed to be done, and how to get it done. People listened to and followed them. To this day, the words they spoke, their ideas, are followed by millions of people around the world.

Pastor Andy Stanley articulated it so well when he said we value integrity, but we follow clarity. Integrity should be a given, like wearing clothes. We don't need anyone to tell us why integrity is important. Clarity, on the other hand, is not a given, and so many people go through life with a lack of it. When relationships are broken, when expectations are not met, when people can't seem to get what they are looking for, it's often due to a lack of clarity. Let me give you a few common examples.

Looking for a new job. I often get approached by people I know in the fundraising world asking for advice or help on getting a new job, finding a new career, or starting a new business. My first question is, "Do you have clarity on what you are looking for, and are you able to communicate that to others in a succinct and confident way?" I see so many generic resumes and cover letters that are vague and uninspiring. You need to be very clear on what you want, then be very intentional about pursuing that opportunity. Your cover letters and resumes should reflect that. I promise yours will stand out from the pile of vague, wishy-washy ones. To help you get clarity on that next job, figure out the answers to these questions and communicate them with conviction:

- What does management and leadership want?

- What skills do you have that will enable them to accomplish what they are looking to do?

- What problem will you solve?

- What's your why? And by that, I mean: Why do you do this work or want to do something else?

Gift officer underperforming. How many times do you hear a manager complaining that their gift officers are not making enough donor calls and visits? Anytime I hear that, I first ask the manager if he or she has clarity on how many calls and visits they should be making. Some shops have visit goals, but very few have phone call goals. As a manager, you need to be very clear on how many calls each of your gift officers needs to make every week, and you need to lead your team to meet or exceed those goals.

Knowing your why. Why would donors want to do more? Why should they care? You must be so clear on that. Once you have absolute clarity around your why, you can convey that message to people with such conviction and intention. That will get people's attention. Don't forget to ask the donor his or her why first.

Clarity is magnetic. When you have clarity and you can convey that, people will notice.

 IF YOU REMEMBER NOTHING ELSE:

✓ If you are not clear on what you want and need, how can you expect others to know?

✓ People follow clarity.

SECTION III:
SKILLSETS

As fundraisers, one of the most important aspects of our work is how we communicate with people. How well we communicate can make the difference between a donor making larger gifts to us versus giving to another charity. Why? Because when we are great communicators, we do a better job of listening, we ask better questions, we build trust more quickly, and we treat donors the way they want to be treated. In this section, we'll discuss ideas on how to take our communication skills to a much deeper level. Your initial reaction might be, "Well, I am good at that already." Being a good communicator is one thing. Being a great communicator—well, that's what separates average performers from top performers.

CHAPTER 19:

ADAPTING YOUR STYLE

So much of learning in schools and in society focuses on developing a higher IQ. Well, in my humble opinion, I think EQ is even more important. *Psychology Today* defines emotional intelligence (EI) or emotional quotient (EQ) as "the ability to identify and manage your own emotions and the emotions of others. It is generally said to include three skills: emotional awareness; the ability to harness emotions and apply them to tasks like thinking and problem solving; and the ability to manage emotions, which includes regulating your own emotions and cheering up or calming down other people."[8]

Having a higher EQ will help us build trust, develop stronger relationships, and get better results in all areas of life. We need to develop a strong sensitivity to how we and others take in the world and communicate. We all have different preferences and styles. With a deeper

---

8. https://www.psychologytoday.com/basics/emotional-intelligence

understanding of those differences, we can adapt our own style to build a deeper connection with others. There are several personality profile programs, such as DISC and Myers-Briggs, that were developed many years ago. Brian Saber of Asking Matters and his friend Andrea Kihlstedt developed their own version of this for fundraisers. It's a simplified version of the DISC and Myers-Briggs models, and I find it a lot easier to remember. They call it Asking Styles, and it transcends fundraising. The model is split into two main components. The first is based on whether you tend to be more introverted or extroverted. That speaks to where you derive your energy: from others or from within. When you are working on a project or solving a problem, do you prefer to figure it out on your own or ask others for help? Do you love meeting people or do you enjoy your privacy? The other component is based on how you take in and process information, analytically or intuitively. Analytic people love details; they think things through before deciding or speaking. Intuitives tend to think big-picture and make decisions quickly.

While everyone possesses some of the traits and styles from each area, we do have dominant styles. For instance, I am an extroverted intuitive. The first step is to appreciate your style and understand that you can be effective no matter what your dominant traits are. Introverts make great fundraisers too! The second step is to learn to recognize the styles of others and adapt your approach to fit the other person's style. Learning this has had a huge impact on my personal and business life.

Here is one of the big lessons I have learned. I used to misinterpret an introvert as someone who was rude or unfriendly. I am not proud to admit it, but before I learned all this, if I were walking my dog in our neighborhood and I passed a neighbor who did not reply to my hello, I got so upset. I would say hello, and if they did not respond I would have a conversation with myself out loud, pretending they were asking me questions. I would say things like "I am great, thanks for asking," and "Yes, it is a beautiful day. Hey, great chatting with you," then walk away in disgust. I am not proud of that, but I took it personally, not realizing that they were either painfully shy or introverted and did not derive energy from others as I do. They simply had their own way of taking in the world and interacting with others. Or maybe they'd had a bad day and just did not feel like engaging.

I was at a concert with my friend Andrei. At the intermission, I went to the restroom; on the way back to the theater, I ran into someone I knew casually. This guy was incredibly shy and introverted. The conversation felt so awkward. I was scrambling for anything to say. It was all I could do to quickly end the exchange and get back to my seat. Upon my return, Andrei asked me where I had been. I told him I ran into someone I knew and how "painful" the conversation was. Andrei looked at me and asked, "Well, if you as an extrovert were so uncomfortable, how do you think he felt? Sounds like he is an introvert and was really struggling." That hit me like a 2×4 to the forehead. Wow, how many times have I made it about me? I did nothing to make that person more comfortable. I did not adapt my style to his. I made up this story that he was a rude person or that he did not like me when all along he was just painfully shy and did not connect to people like I did. Who knows what kind of conversation we could have had if I had been more empathetic to his style and preferences for communicating? A big lesson learned indeed.

Here is an example of how I apply this understanding in my fundraising work. One of my larger donors, whom I will call Tony, is clearly an introverted analytic. Tony is a financial advisor. He is not big on the small talk and loves metrics, reports, and data. It did not take me a whole lot of time to learn that about Tony. With that understanding, I knew to limit my small talk. After asking lots of questions to determine what was most important to Tony, it was clear that he wanted to see the metrics, our 990, our charity navigator report, and impact reports on his gifts. As an extroverted intuitive, I had to work harder to focus on the details and limit the touchy-feely stuff with Tony. With conscious effort and focus on Tony's needs, we connected pretty quickly, and Tony continues to be a very generous and happy donor.

How do you determine if your donor is a big-picture thinker or wants to see more detail? Ask them. You can say something like "Some donors I work with want to see the details and metrics, while others are bigger picture and want to hear stories of impact. Which do you prefer?" I use this question all the time, especially when a donor asks me to send them information or a proposal, or when I am presenting my case for giving.

Matching and Mirroring

A lot of this relates to the science of Neuro-Linguistic Programming (NLP). If you are not familiar with it, there are many books and resources online to dig into this deeper. One of my big takeaways from NLP is the art of matching and mirroring. Matching and mirroring is the process of copying or mimicking (in a subtle way) another person's behavior in order to connect with them. It's not about being inauthentic or manipulative; it's about being in sync with the other person. Have you ever been walking down the street with a friend, having a great conversation, and noticed that you were both walking in unison? You're not even aware of it, but you are matching your friend's steps and the way he or she is moving down the street. You can apply that to any interaction with others.

Here are some things you can match and mirror:

Posture. If I am meeting with a donor and he is leaning back in his chair, relaxed, I'll lean back in my chair. If we are sitting side by side at a conference table and she leans into me, I'll follow her and lean in as well. I feel a stronger sense of connection with the person and sense that they do too.

Speech. I tend to talk fast. I have had to adjust my rate of talking with older and more laid-back donors. If I am speaking with a young, successful executive in New York City, I may tend to speak faster than if I am on the phone with an older retiree living in the South. If a donor is a loud talker, I'll increase my volume; if they speak softly, I'll lower my tone.

Vocabulary. This borders on the manipulative side, so I suggest you use it with caution. I tend to only use it with people I know well and who have a sense of humor. I often use it in a light-hearted, humorous way. A donor may play golf and talk about it a lot. In the course (you're thinking golf course, aren't you? See what I did there?) of a conversation, if I am explaining something to them, I might say, "Let me tee that up for you." Corny, I know, but it does get a chuckle. If a donor owns a boat, I might sign off in an e-mail with "Hoping your retirement is smooth sailing." If your donor uses the same phrases and words a lot, you can use those words when communicating back to them. Again, use with caution; we don't want to come across like we are patronizing them.

Touching and contact. Not everyone is comfortable shaking hands or hugging. They may be shy or worried about catching germs. So, when meeting people for the first time, I'll approach them and see if they raise their hand to shake. If they don't, I won't extend mine. I let them make the first move, especially women. Men must be careful when greeting women in a business setting. This goes for hugging too! In business and my personal life, if I see a female friend, client, or donor—someone I know well—I'll let them initiate the hug. This sounds like common sense, but it's another one of those things we take for granted that can turn someone off quickly.

Communication preferences. As technology and the way people communicate evolve, we have to be sensitive to how our donors prefer to communicate. I love to speak on the phone, and I get frustrated with long e-mail exchanges. I had a recent interaction with a Fundraiser for a charity that my wife Lorraine and I are fairly active with. The fundraiser kept e-mailing me to try to resolve the matter. After days of back-and-forth e-mails, I finally e-mailed him back and asked if he could just pick up the phone and call me so we could get the matter resolved. From that point on, I noticed he never picked up the phone to call me. It was always e-mails. I am not trying to say he's wrong. Chances are he is not getting the training that his employer should be giving him. He is young and does not know any better. We should simply ask donors how they prefer to communicate and match that preference. You can ask, "Do you prefer I call you or e-mail?" Also, take every opportunity to get in front of a donor.

So, what is your style? What are those subtle things you are doing that may be limiting your ability to connect with people? It all starts with deeper self (and other) awareness.

To learn more about your style preferences, go to www.askingmatters.com. There you can take the Asking Styles test. It's quick and incredibly helpful.

IF YOU REMEMBER NOTHING ELSE:

✓ Not everyone thinks and communicates as you do. Adapt your style and approach to the styles of others.

✓ Ask donors how they would like be contacted—by phone, e-mail, or some other method.

CHAPTER 20:
LISTENING

Listen not to respond but to understand.

A classical pianist must be great at reading music. An NFL running back must be a fast sprinter. A New York City cop must be good at making decisions quickly. Fundraisers must be exceptional listeners. It's one more skillset that we take for granted. We tell ourselves we are good listeners. Of course we're good listeners. We must be. It's fundamentally essential to our work. We listen to develop relationships and further our organization's mission. But according to Tony Alessandra, most of us are not exactly overachieving. The normal, untrained listener is likely to understand and retain only about 50 percent of a conversation, and this relatively poor percentage drops to an even less impressive 25 percent retention rate forty-eight hours later. That's good, but certainly nowhere near great. Which leads up to the obvious: How can we be great listeners?

The better we are at listening, the more trust we build with donors, and the more we can connect our donor's needs with the needs of those we serve.

"Listen for what's different." It's become my mantra.

Let's face it, for those of us who have been doing the same work for years, after a while we can almost predict what our donor is going to say. Many of us think we've heard it all. But we haven't. That's why we all need to listen for what's different. Before every donor phone call or visit, before you pick up that phone or get out of your car, take a minute to reflect and ask yourself, "What can I learn in this conversation that I don't already know; that I have never heard before?"

One of my favorite Jeff Bridges movies is *Starman*. I know you are thinking *The Big Lebowski*. Agreed, but *Starman* is my second favorite. In the film, Bridges (Starman) comes to Earth from another planet, then meets and falls in love with Jenny Hayden, played by Karen Allen. Starman listens with an almost religious zeal to people explaining normal, everyday things. After ingesting this information, one of his character's recurring lines is "Define _____."

Here is a sample from the movie script:

> *[Starman and Jenny are looking at a dead deer strapped to the hood of a car]*
> **Deer Hunter**: *Cried when you saw Bambi?*
> **Starman**: *Define "Bambi"?*
> **Deer Hunter**: *Huh?*
> **Jenny Hayden**: *He doesn't understand, he's not from around here.*
> **Deer Hunter**: *[laughs] You don't speaking English,*

huh? Heh-hey!
[walks away snickering]
Jenny Hayden*: [to Starman] Steer clear of that bozo.*
Starman*: Define "bozo"?*
Jenny Hayden*: Jerk.*

That's how inquisitive we should be with donors. So insatiably curious about their stories and what's important to them that we can't help but listen for what's different. Now, we certainly don't want to annoy the donor by asking them to explain everything they say, but how many times does a donor say something that we may not fully understand, and rather than ask for further definition, we nod our head in agreement? Here is an example. The donor says, "The nurses and doctors at your hospital were so accommodating." You may respond with, "Oh, I am so glad to hear that." Or you may dig deeper. What does accommodating mean? Ask them. "When you say accommodating, what do you mean?" This will take the conversation to a deeper level.

So many times, we keep the conversation at a surface level when there is an opportunity to go deeper. My wife and I used to go to the Caribbean islands every year. I love the ocean and fish but get horribly seasick. (Yes, I have tried Dramamine and the patches. They have never worked for me.) We went snorkeling every chance we got. Well, the snorkeling was great, but staying on the surface limited what we saw, what we discovered. We would come back to the resort and talk to someone who had gone scuba diving that day. They saw and discovered so much more than we did. Why? Because they went deeper, well below the surface. Always strive to take your conversations to a deeper level.

While studying for my CAP® (Chartered Advisor in Philanthropy) certification, I learned about the Four Levels of Listening by Otto Scharmer. No chapter on listening would be complete without some mention of it. Listening seems to be an abstract thing. How can you measure how well you are listening? Scharmer teaches us that there are different levels of listening, and each level takes us deeper and deeper. Here is a summary of those levels:

1. Downloading—This is where most listening is done. I view this type of listening as being polite. You reconfirm what you already know or think you know.

2. Factual—We access what we notice as different. What is different from what I thought they were going to say? Listening for what's different.

3. Empathic Listening—This is listening with an open heart. Listening through the eyes of the other person. It's not about facts and figures; it's about connecting on an emotional level.

4. Generative or Emergent—Scharmer describes this level as "Connecting to the emerging future—to a future possibility that links to your emerging self; to who you really are."[9] Scharmer also says in his book *TheoryU: Leading from the Future as It Emerges*, "We no longer empathize with someone in front of us. We are in an altered state—maybe 'communion' or 'grace' is the word

9. https://www.presencing.com/theoryu

that comes closest to the texture of this experience that refuses to be dragged onto the surface of words."

While this all sounds cerebral, I am convinced that this is where the larger, ultimate gifts come from. A level of listening where we and the donor are imagining that anything is possible—that we can abolish world hunger, find the cure for ALS, change our students' lives. Strive for Level 4 listening whenever possible!

Okay, so how do we get great at listening? Here are five ways:

- Practice yoga or meditation—This is all about learning to be present. To quiet down the noise in your mind. It's called practice for a reason. You can train yourself to be more present with people. This is a great way to do that and reduce stress in your life.

- Stop making it about you—Every time you find yourself drifting away from what the other person is saying, catch yourself and keep telling yourself, "It's not about me; it's not about me." Yes, we need to make our budgets and raise money. That will come if we focus on the donor first.

- Dominate the listening—I love when a donor says to me "Joe, I am doing all the talking here." I respond with, "My job is to dominate the listening."

- Catch, then pitch—This is an old sales concept I learned many years ago. "Catch" refers to gathering information. I don't make my case or a sales pitch until I have done as much catching of information from the prospect as possible. I strive to be Johnny Bench (Baseball

Hall of Famer, catcher for the Cincinnati Reds), Jerry Rice (San Francisco 49ers, Raiders, and Seahawks receiver), and Eddie Ward (master trapeze artist of the early twentieth century) all rolled up into one. I am a master at catching.

- Wait to respond—This is a big one. Living in the Northeast, where life goes at a faster pace, I am surprised by how many times I hear people interrupt someone else while they are speaking. I have not perfected this myself. There are times, usually when I am excited by the conversation, when I will interrupt someone. I do my best to catch myself, apologize, and ask the other person to continue. Be conscious of how often you are doing that. Wait until the person has stopped talking. Give it a few seconds. Then respond.

Quick Tip

Next time you go to a crowded restaurant with a donor, and the greeter brings you to a table, if you have a choice between sitting in the chair facing a wall or the crowded restaurant, let your donor face the wall. They will be less likely to be distracted because all they can see is you. You, being the trained listener, will have an easier time not getting distracted by all the noise and commotion in the restaurant.

So, I ask you: What can you hear that you have never heard before? I suspect plenty.

Joseph Tumolo

 IF YOU REMEMBER NOTHING ELSE:

✓ Listen to understand, not to respond.

✓ Slow down.

✓ Dominate the listening.

CHAPTER 21:

ASKING BETTER QUESTIONS

"If I had an hour to solve a problem and my life depended on the solution, I would spend the first fifty-five minutes determining the proper question to ask…for once I know the proper question, I could solve the problem in less than five minutes."
— *Albert* Einstein

While donors are not problems, Einstein saw the value of developing better questions. From the time we are five years old, we are told how important it is to know the answers. We are trained to think that it's only about having all the answers. Yet the power is often not in the answer, but in the question. No one ever teaches us how to ask better questions. Self-development guru Tony Robbins tells us that successful people ask better questions and thus get better answers.

It's not always how much we know, but our ability to ask better questions that separates us from all the mediocre fundraisers out there. Great questions, asked with sincerity and authenticity, show donors we care enough to want to learn more, that we are committed to doing what's best for the donor.

In the context of fundraising, there are several types of questions we can ask. The first are us-centered and donor-centered. Us-centered questions are mostly aimed at what type and amount of gift a donor may want to make. These questions are important and should be asked appropriately. If all we ask are us-centered questions, however, we never fully understand what our donor's concerns, hopes, and goals around giving are.

I was reminded of the importance of asking the right types of questions the last time I bought a car. I was in no hurry, so I visited five car dealerships that sold different brands of cars. None of the salespeople I met asked me anything but us-centered questions. You know the ones: "Are you looking to buy or lease? Do you have a car to trade in? Are you looking to buy a car today?" Those are all us-centered questions that help the salesperson, not the buyer. No one asked me questions about my needs, like "What do you do for a living? Do you drive long distances? Do you need lots of room to carry equipment? What do you like and dislike about the car you currently own? What's most important to you in deciding what kind of car to purchase?" These are questions that help me meet my goals. (To be clear, selling cars is a great way to make a living. There are great car salespeople. Many, however, are mediocre at best. It's not their fault; they are often not properly trained.) How often do we do this with our donors? Yes, we need to ask those us-centered questions, but only after we have asked donor-centered questions first.

Let's figure out why our donors want to do something and the impact they want to have—then we can figure out how.

To give you an idea of how the questions differ, here is a short list of us-centered versus donor-centered questions. There are hundreds more!

Us-Centered Questions:

What other charities do you support?

Of your top five favorite charities, where do we stand?

What one thing do you feel we can do to improve the services we provide?

Who else is involved in deciding what charities you support?

Donor-Centered Questions:

Why are you so loyal to our organization?

Do you have a good understanding of how we are investing your donations?

Do you have goals around your giving/philanthropy?

If money were no object, what would you like to see happen with our program?

What one thing can we do to be better stewards of your donations?

By the way, when asking someone for feedback, we often ask, "How can we improve?" Most times, the person will reply with, "I cannot think of anything." When we rephrase the question as, "What one thing can we do to improve?" it encourages the person to come up with an answer. We need to be judicious with when and to whom we ask donor-centered questions. These types of questions are best received by donors with whom we have a relationship that is based on trust. The last thing we ever want to hear from a donor is "That's none of your business." Ask your donors for permission to ask these types of questions. You can let them know that very few people in our business take the time to ask donors these types of questions, and that the answers to these types of questions will ensure that they accomplish what they want with their giving.

Exercise: Write down your top five donor-centered questions. Do they inspire you? How can you improve them?

The next types of questions are open-ended versus closed-ended. Closed-ended questions are answered generally with a yes, no, or I don't know. An example in the fundraising world is, "Will you consider a gift of $10,000 to help fund our new children's program?" Great question, but it's easy for the donor to say no. Then where do you go from there? Sure, you can ask if it's just no for now or no never, and you can ask further questions to learn more—and you should. You can also ask for that gift with an open-ended question. Open-ended questions generally start with when, how, why, where, or what. Asking for a gift with an open-ended question might sound something like "How would you feel about a conversation around increasing your gift to $10,000 to help fund our new children's program?" You must use your own judgment based on your relationship with the donor and the circumstances.

The takeaway is to think before you ask, and if appropriate, make it an open-ended question.

 IF YOU REMEMBER NOTHING ELSE:

"Quality questions create a quality life. Successful people ask better questions, and as a result, they get better answers."
– Tony Robbins

CHAPTER 22:

GETTING THE VISIT

"Life is a series of presentations."

– Tony Jeary

In my work with thousands of fundraisers, the biggest challenge I hear is that it's hard to get the visit. I sometimes struggle with getting the visit as well. Donors ignore our messages or they e-mail us back with short messages that say "No need to visit, everything is good." It's not easy. If it were easy, our organizations would not need us. I remind myself of that when I am having one of those days where no one seems to respond.

The first step is to craft your messages carefully. I have seen people spend weeks and even months writing and refining copy for marketing materials, carefully examining every word, passing proofs around to anyone with a pulse. So much time and energy is invested. Marketing is expensive, it is a reflection on your organization, and it should be done the right way. But what about your voicemails and e-mails?

Think of the last presentation you gave. No doubt you were prepared. You knew what you were going to say and what you wanted your audience to take away. Your goal was to inform, persuade, and/or inspire them. Hopefully it included a clear call to action: what you wanted the audience to do because of your talk. Now, think of the last voicemail or e-mail you sent. Were you equally prepared with your message? Did you know what you were going to say and what you wanted the recipient to know or do? Did you spend time working on that message? Did you refine it so it flowed smoothly? Was it compelling?

Our donors are getting calls from lots of other charities. What will you say that will separate you from the rest of the pack and encourage your donor to visit?

Here are some guidelines for developing voicemail script outlines to help you get more donor visits.

Keep it short. In this fast-paced world, it's more important than ever to keep our messages short and to the point. Look at Twitter, Facebook, and current website design. They all use snippets of information, not wordy and drawn-out messaging. Most people have the attention span of a hummingbird on Starbucks coffee. We are all bombarded with lots of messages, solicitations, and requests for our time and money from all areas of our lives. You must make your point quickly. I suggest you keep your voicemails under sixty seconds and your e-mails less than three paragraphs. I could go on, but...

Focus on the recipient. Your message should be all about the other person, not about you and your agenda.

"You" should be used more than "I" or "we." Instead of saying "I want to come out and visit you," you can say, "I think you would enjoy or benefit from a visit because…"

Stress the benefit to the donor and those you serve. This is a huge point, and I find it to be one of the most challenging components of a message. How will the donor benefit from a phone conversation or visit? "You might find it helpful if I update you on how we are investing your donation and the impact it's having here on campus."

Include a clear call to action. What is the result you are looking for? If you are calling a donor to set up a visit, say it right up front. "Hi Mrs. Howell, I am calling (or reaching out to) you today to set a time for us to visit." Depending on what stage you are at with your donor, you may even tell them you are calling to set up a visit to talk about making a gift, how they might want to support the campaign, or something similar.

Say it with enthusiasm and passion. Your voicemails need to be upbeat and oozing with enthusiasm. Not so much that it comes across as phony, but just enough for the recipient to think, "Hmm, this sounds like someone whom I could hang out with." People like dealing with happy, passionate people. Make sure that comes through in your message.

Write it out. Write out a voicemail script and practice it until you have it memorized. After you practice it enough, you'll internalize it, and it will sound natural. Great actors practice their lines until they sound natural and spontaneous. Think of Meryl Streep. The dialogue she delivers was written by someone else, yet it sounds like she is speaking those words for the very first time because she has practiced and internalized them until they sound natural and convincing.

Record yourself. This is tough. I hate hearing myself on the playback, but it's incredibly helpful. Every time I listen back to my recorded messages, I find new ways to make the message more concise and impactful. Leave yourself voicemails with your new message. Keep refining it until it's just where you want it.

Get everyone on board. If you are managing gift officers, do you know what they are saying on their phone calls, voicemails, and e-mails? Are they sending the message you want them to send?

Here is a sample of a typical voicemail that I use to set up a visit with a donor.

Hello Lorraine:

This is Joe from the Foundation for Follicly Challenged Men. I am calling to set up a time for you, Mike, and me to visit because I was looking at your gift records today and saw that you have been giving for over ten years. Other donors are telling me that they are benefiting from a visit to be thanked personally, updated on the impact of their gifts, and to provide feedback on how we can be better stewards of their donations.

I will send you an e-mail follow-up as well. Our visit should take about forty-five minutes unless you and Mike have lots of questions. Would you let me know your availability to visit the week of January third or suggest another week if that one does

not work for you? You can reach me here at 610-653-7906. And my name is Joe Tumolo with the Foundation for Follicly Challenged Men.
If you are not able to get back to me, I'll circle back next week.
I look forward to connecting with you, Lorraine. Thanks to you and Mike for your continued support in our work.

Some comments about this message:

- I let them know how long the visit should take. Most people can spend forty-five minutes. This relieves the donor of any concerns about our visit taking up too much of their time.

- I alter this based on the how well I know the donor.

- I always let them know what happens next. If the donor is not able to get back to me, I let them know I will keep trying until we connect.

- I try to include any other decision maker (spouse, partner, caretaker, etc.) in the visit.

- This is a guideline. Everyone has their own style. What I say may not exactly fit your approach. If you like this script, adapt it to your personality.

Exercise: Set up a few hours to meet with your team. Work on a script outline for phone calls, voicemails, and e-mails. Practice and role-play among the group. Everyone has their own style, but they should all be sending the same message containing the five key components outlined above.

Managing a Nonresponsive Donor

Often, you'll continue to try to reach a donor with no response. What do you do to get them to respond? How long do you keep trying? The last thing you want to do is irritate a donor. And the more time you spend chasing a disinterested donor, the less time you have for those donors who are open to a visit. The solution? Have a policy for how many attempts you and your team will make to reach a donor. Now, if the donor is a major or leadership donor, you might allow for a higher number of attempts. Second, decide what each attempt looks like. How many voicemails, how many e-mails or letters?

Here is an example of a written process for a five-attempt approach for reaching a donor:

- Attempt 1—Leave a voicemail and send an e-mail.

- Attempt 2—Attempt to reach, do not leave voicemail or e-mail.

- Attempt 3—Attempt to reach, do not leave voicemail or e-mail.

- Attempt 4—Mail survey (as discussed in Chapter 14).

- Attempt 5—Final voicemail and e-mail.

Third, get creative. How can you reach that person? I know a fundraiser who will stop at a donor's house with no appointment, and drop off a small gift from the college. He has never had a donor get offended. I would be impressed if someone had the courage and commitment to show up at my door.

Here are some other ideas you can try to help you connect.

Forget trying to get the visit. Say what? Yes, forget about trying to get the visit right away. People are busy. Instead, see if the donor is open to an initial ten-minute phone conversation. Once you get them on the phone, your job is to keep them on the phone as long as you can (provided they are engaged in the conversation). The longer you stay on the phone with the donor, the more likely you are to build trust. If the call is going well, then you can ask for the visit.

Another approach for completely unresponsive donors is to see if they have a LinkedIn profile. Look at their connections to see if you or anyone in your organization knows one of those connections well enough to call them and see if they can assist in reaching your donor. Mail a funny card. Have someone else in your office (or a board member) attempt to reach the person. A different voice might resonate better with the donor.

If nothing else works, leave them a final voicemail that sounds something like this:

> *Hi, Lorraine. It's Joe Tumolo, calling back from The Foundation for Follicly Challenged Men. Gee, I feel like I am stalking you. The last thing I want to do is be a nuisance. I have been trying to connect with you because you are important to us and the men we serve. Sounds like it's just not a great time. Please know we are very grateful for your support. Should your schedule change and you are open to a visit or even a quick phone conversation, please let me*

know. Thanks so much. Again, it's Joe Tumolo and my number is 610-653-7906.

There is no silver bullet for getting the visit every time, but we need to do everything we can to increase our odds. Having a process keeps you from chasing the same donors over and over. You can always circle back to the non-responders. Realize that there are some donors who just don't want to do more. They are perfectly content giving what they are giving but don't want to talk about doing more. There are others who no longer want to give, and there are still others who are open to doing more. Our job is to find the ones who want to do more and build relationships with them.

 IF YOU REMEMBER NOTHING ELSE:

✓ Be intentional about your voicemails. Refine them, make them as compelling as possible.

✓ Sometimes you are better off going for a ten-minute phone conversation versus a visit.

✓ Have a process for the number of times you are going to try to reach a donor.

CHAPTER 23:

WHAT'S YOUR MESSAGE?

"The message of you is your brand. It is what you stand for. It's what you are famous for or want to be famous for. It's your life's work as well as the lessons you have already learned. It's what you will be remembered for when you die. It's your legacy."

— Judy Carter, from her book
The Message of You

Much has been written and spoken around the importance of stories in fundraising. Author Christina Baldwin teaches us the power of stories with her simple phrase: "Words are how we think. Stories are how we link." Most fundraisers spend their time gathering and telling stories of others—donors, people who benefit from their work, and people who do great work to forward the mission. Little time is spent on crafting their own story. Our personal story is equally as important as the stories of others. When we can deliver our personal story and message in a clear, compelling way, it will motivate others to join us.

For the longest time, I did not think I had a story or a message that was all that compelling. I thought I had to have a rags-to-riches story or a story that spoke of going to hell and back to be of any interest to others. For years, I sat in the audiences watching other people stand and tell their stories, wishing I had one to tell. Finally, after much research, I learned I do have my own story. We all do. It's what makes us unique. Everyone else's stories aren't better; they are just different.

If you are not sure what your unique message or story is, here are some concepts I have learned over the years that might help you.

What's Your Why?

Why do you do what you do? Why are you so committed to the cause? How can you inspire others to join you?

Author and speaker Simon Sinek did a TED Talk called "Start with Why." You can find the talk along with a five-minute edited version on YouTube.[10] If you have not seen it, check it out. It has had a dramatic impact on me; I share it with all my clients and audiences. Sinek's basic premise is that most people focus on what they do and how they do it. Very few talk about why they do what they do. This goes for fundraisers, salespeople, marketers, politicians, and more. Sinek urges us to get very clear on our why, and

10. https://www.youtube.com/watch?v=IPYeCltXpxw

to always lead with that. Why do you do what you do, and why should anyone care? Here is a practical example for sharing your why:

You are at a networking meeting. Everyone around the table takes turns introducing themselves. Most will talk about what they do. "I am an attorney" or "I am the director of alumni." What you won't likely hear is people saying why they do what they do. You will stand out by starting with your why.

When it's your turn, you can sound like everyone else by saying, "I am a major gifts officer for Third World Missions." Or you can inspire those in the room by starting with your why. "There are so many children in third-world countries who, from birth, are destined to live a life in poverty. Yes, there are many children who live in poverty in this country, but most have resources, like government assistance, available to them. Kids in these other countries have nothing. Most people see their plight and brush it off by saying that's a shame, then get on with their lives. We at Third World Missions dedicate our lives to giving these kids the education and tools they need to live healthy, productive lives."

The why is your story. It's personal. It's why you get out of bed in the morning. It's why you make the sacrifices you do. It's why you gave up that job that paid twice as much as what you make now to do the life-changing work you do. Figure out your why, memorize it, live it, and share it with your donors.

Ideas for Crafting Simple, Compelling Messages

There are simple ways to structure your message so that it's concise, compelling, and memorable. They work for marketing materials (postcards, brochures, case statements), sixty-second presentations, or eighteen-minute talks.

CAR method. In my book *Simplify, A Simple Approach to Building a Sustainable Planned Giving Program*, I talk about my experiences helping my church start a planned giving program. A few weeks after we officially launched the program, I was walking into church when the pastor asked me to get up and give a quick ninety-second commercial for our new legacy society. I had less than fifteen minutes to prepare. What could I say that was concise, compelling, and would inspire people to take action? Fortunately, I learned the CAR method of crafting a story or message. CAR stands for

C–Context

A–Action

R–Result.

Allow me to explain.

Context—An introduction of what the story or message is about. It gives people the background, the people involved, and in the context of fundraising, introduces a problem or opportunity.

Action—What happened or needs to happen in the story or message.

Result—The outcome, the moral of the story, the take-away. The result needs to inspire your donor to want to do more, to take action.

So, my ninety-second message went something like this:

Context—Thanks to your generous support, the church is thriving. The impact we are having on our families and the less fortunate in our community has never been stronger. While we are financially sound, we do need to be prepared for the future. Most churches that thrive and sustain have a strong endowment. Ours has room for lots of growth.

Action—To help build our endowment, we have launched the Living Water Legacy Society. Our goal is to add twenty-five charter members to our legacy society this year. Please join my wife and me as founding members of the Living Water Society. My contact information is in this brochure and the church directory.

Result—The Living Water society will help us grow our endowment so that the great work we are doing will continue for your children, their children, and generations to come.

Here is another example of a story using the CAR method:

Context—Let me tell you about this incredible student I met. Manny is an imposing guy who at first glance comes across as someone you do not want to make mad. After hearing Manny speak for just a few seconds, you realize that he has a heart of gold and you cannot help but be inspired by his story. Manny grew up on the streets; he was a tough kid and got in a lot of trouble. Manny ended up in prison. It was there that he turned his life around and decided to get on the right path. After his release, he found it hard adjusting to his newfound freedom. He struggled to maintain a job and wound up homeless. He began to think about going back to school, something he had always wanted to do.

<u>Action</u>—Manny enrolled in the local community college, and with the help of financial aid, was well on his way. Unfortunately, Manny struggled with his grades and failed his first semester. He had to maintain a minimum grade level to keep his financial aid. Manny found a friend in Ann, who worked as a student advisor. Ann believed in Manny and agreed to tutor him to help him get back on track.

<u>Result</u>—Manny turned his grades around, stayed on financial aid, and graduated from the community college. He now lives in his own apartment and has a great job at the local hospital. In his spare time, Manny works with young adults who struggle as he did. It's through the generosity of loyal donors that people like Manny have life-changing experiences and go on to live extraordinary lives.

Now don't you want to just take out your wallet and support people like Manny?

Nine-word story. This is a fun exercise to do with a group. You need to reduce your story (your why) into three lines consisting of three words per line. Here is one I made up for an organization near and dear to my heart, The Make-A-Wish Foundation.

Kids need hope.

We grant wishes.

Dreams come true.

What, so what, now what? This is one of my new favorites. The answers to these three simple questions make a great case, message, and call to action.

What?—What is the challenge?

So what?—This is our why. Why we do what we do.

Now what?—What needs to be done, and how can people help?

Here is an example:

<u>What</u>—Opiate addiction is an epidemic spiraling out of control. Families are being torn apart, and people are dying at an alarming rate.

<u>So what? (Why?)</u>—These families need counseling, support, and the tools to get straight and live happy, fulfilling lives.

<u>Now what?</u>—Please consider a gift to help us build a state-of-the-art treatment center this year.

Quick Tip

Delivering compelling, clear messages and stories will separate you from most other fundraisers in the marketplace. You'll get people's attention and inspire many to take action to get the outcome you desire.

Learn story telling from the best. Check out www.themoth. org and www.ted.com.

 IF YOU REMEMBER NOTHING ELSE:

✓ Start with why.

✓ People don't care what you do. They care *why* you do.

✓ Have a system for telling your stories.

CHAPTER 24:

MAKING THE ASK

Don't make decisions for your donors.

What fundraising book would be complete without a chapter on making the ask? Now, there are plenty of great books and online resources on how to ask for gifts. Here are a few of my higher-level thoughts on asking for gifts.

First, here's my perspective as a donor. My wife Lorraine and I are charitable and philanthropically minded. We have over a dozen charities in our estate plans through our will, retirement plans, and donor-advised fund. I continue to see most of the nonprofits we support take a very reactive approach to asking us for money. If we go back to our annual fund principles, we know that donors have a specific comfort level when they are willing to give, depending on the time of year. If we limit our asks to year-end, we are very likely leaving money on the table. Everyone mails in November and December, and I cannot give to everyone. Sadly, for some of those organizations, they never ask the rest of the year. As a business owner, my cash flow varies month to month. If a charity approaches me in a good month, I am more likely to make a larger gift. What's the best way to know? Ask. Ask your donors if they have goals or a plan around their charitable giving. Do they like to give at certain times of the year? Then set a yearly goal for each of your qualified donors and track it carefully throughout the year.

When was the last time a fundraiser asked you and your significant other to talk about a gift? When I ask that question in my seminars, I'll get just a handful of people raising their hands. Granted, most of us in the fundraising space are not comfortable or able to make the big gifts, but it's clear to me that we are not asked to stretch our giving all that often. And a big gift can mean a lot of things to different charities.

How can I help? Four words we all love hearing from our donor. We don't have to worry about making the perfect ask when the donor does it for us. Now, we need to be intentional and strategic about making the ask, in the right amount, at the right time. I do believe we should do everything we can in the cultivation process to encourage donors to ask us that question—how can I help? That approach separates the amateurs from the pros. Anyone can hard-sell donors, pushing them to donate. I look at it like football versus golf. In football, you can try harder, run faster, hit harder, and chances are, you'll play a better game. With golf, it seems the harder you try, the worse you do. It's not about hitting the ball harder or rushing through the shots. It's about being strategic, taking your time, and playing with finesse. It takes careful planning, intentional cultivation, and building trust to get to the point where donors close themselves. Let's not rely on them to close themselves, but let's do everything we can to make the ask a rewarding and pleasant conversation for everyone.

When Do I Bring Up the Gift Conversation?

This is an area of our work that sparks much discussion among fundraising professionals. Let's say you have an unassigned donor who has been giving $50 a year for over ten years. Your goal is to visit that donor, thank them, learn about why they give, and, at some point, ask them to do more. Do you plan to ask for a gift on the first visit? Do you let her know you are going to ask? Do you tell her you are not going to ask on the first visit? The answers to these questions depend on a lot of things, but it's really important to be intentional about whatever you decide.

Donors are not naïve. They know fundraisers aren't paid just to visit them and exchange pleasantries. They know our job is to raise as much money as we can for those we serve. You may consider letting the donor know while you are setting up the visit whether you plan to ask them for a gift. If you are in the camp of "never ask for a gift on the first visit," I suggest you tell the donor that, but let them know that if they decide to make a gift when you are together, that would be great too. You can say this when setting the visit or as soon as you get in front of the donor. You can say something like, "My reason for visiting with you today was not to ask you for a gift, unless you decide that you are ready to do so." If you leave out the "unless you decide that you are ready to do so," you are not letting the donor make her own choices. Maybe she was thrilled you came to see her and was ready to make a gift.

What's your asking style? In Chapter 19, I talked about my friend Brian Saber. Check out Brian's site (www.asking-matters.com) for lots of great tools and ideas on getting better at making the ask.

 IF YOU REMEMBER NOTHING ELSE:

✓ Many donors will give more but are never asked to do so.

✓ You have donors who have never been asked for a gift face-to-face.

✓ Don't make decisions for your donors.

CHAPTER 25:

HELP PEOPLE DECIDE

Have you ever found yourself chasing a donor? You had a great conversation. The donor said they were interested, agreed to another conversation, and then nothing. Radio silence. Perhaps you have had multiple conversations with a donor. He has asked for multiple proposals or gift illustrations. You are more than happy to help him, but you are starting to feel as though he will never make a decision. At some point, you need to have a conversation with him about what he needs to see to help him decide what he would like to do. To be clear, I am not suggesting that we ever hard-sell or strong-arm a donor into making a gift. I am saying that as responsible fundraisers, we need to keep filling the pipeline and qualifying donors (ABQ). That requires us to keep moving donors along and finding new ones. I am suggesting that we give the donor an "out" if they are not feeling enthusiastic and inspired to make the gift.

People don't make decisions for lots of reasons. They have not been shown the true benefit of investing their money for the gift, product, or service. They have pre-buyer's remorse and are embarrassed to tell us or admit to themselves they don't want to move ahead. There are many other reasons. So, why not give donors the option to say no? You can say something like "Barbara, we are so grateful for your support and your interest in wanting to do more. It does sound like (or feels like) this is not a good time for you to be doing this. Why don't we put this on the shelf for now, and we can revisit it when you are ready?"

I would say that over 50 percent of the time, the prospect, client, or donor will respond to that with "No, no, I want to do this, let's get it done." Most people think that salespeople and fundraisers only want to hear yes. Sure, we want and need as many yesses as we can get. But the next best thing to a yes is a no. Life is too short to chase think-it-overs. One of the most memorable concepts I learned as a young sales guy was to let people know it's okay to say no. It lowers their defenses and builds trust faster.

Should We?

I was in a restaurant with my wife and another couple. We sat down and the waiter served us each a drink. About half an hour later, the waiter came to our table and asked, "Should I be asking you if you would like another round?" I am not sure if he said it that way to prevent the liability of serving too much alcohol (although we had only had one drink), or whether he even gave much thought to how he said it, but it resonated with me. I quickly got my phone out and e-mailed a note to myself that said "should we?"

I thought, what a great way to pose a question when we are concerned that we may be pressing too hard with a donor. I had been cultivating a church member to make a planned gift to the church. She had told me three months prior that she was interested in chatting. I followed up with her as she requested, but I never heard back from her. I tried a few times, but nothing. I saw her in church one day. She approached me and said, "I know I told you I was interested in doing something, but I have been busy." I replied with, "No problem; **should we** talk about setting up a time to visit?" She of course replied with a yes and made a gift! On planned giving visits, there are many times when, after a donor has gone on and on about how much our organization means to him, I will simply respond with "Based on everything you told me today, Rick, **should we** be having a conversation about other ways to support our work? Ways that cost you nothing now?"

✍ IF YOU REMEMBER NOTHING ELSE:

- ✓ Help your donors make a decision.
- ✓ Let them know it's okay to say no.

CHAPTER 26:

CLEAR FUTURE

You just had this amazing donor visit. You hit it off with the donor. They were gushing about you and your organization. They were all fired up about a gift conversation. You left the meeting and got back to your office. Your boss or colleague asked you how the visit went, and you told them how well it went and that the donor was interested. Your colleague then asks what happens next. You have no idea. In all the excitement, you forgot to set clear next steps with the donor. We have all done it. I often see this with untrained salespeople. They come to the house to talk about a project or service and give an estimate to do the work. Oftentimes, they leave with no idea what their next steps are.

This is another life lesson I learned from the Sandler Sales Training program. Always have a clear future when leaving a donor visit or hanging up the phone with them. A clear future means you both know exactly what's going to happen next—who is doing what and when, and what happens if one person does not hear from the other.

To help me remember to get a clear future with a donor, I created what's known in the science of neuro-linguistic programming as an anchor. In NLP, "anchoring" refers to the process of associating an internal response or thought with some external or physical trigger. Here is an example. Close your eyes and think of a peaceful place. It could be a deserted beach or a green meadow with blues skies and the perfect temperature. Feel yourself in that scene. Notice the sights and sounds and smells. Now, take your left thumb and forefinger and gently pinch the area between your thumb and forefinger on your right hand. Keep pinching slowly, visualizing the calm, peaceful scene. Repeat this several times a day. After a few weeks of doing this, you will develop a trigger that will enable you to calm yourself down. Every time you get stressed out, gently pinch your right hand. You should begin to feel calm and relaxed.

One of my anchors for making sure the donor and I understand the next step takes place with the goodbye handshake. When my palm makes contact with theirs (external trigger), my brain remembers (internal trigger) to make sure the donor(s) and I both know exactly what happens next. It has become such a habit that I don't always need to shake their hand; I can trigger it on a phone call as well.

What happens next can look like:

- We agree on a specific day and time to chat on the phone as a follow-up.

- You agree to send the donor follow-up material by a certain date and ask them how much time they need before you follow up.

 IF YOU REMEMBER NOTHING ELSE:

✓ Never leave a donor conversation without everyone involved knowing the next steps.

CHAPTER 27:
CHOOSE YOUR WORDS CAREFULLY

I want to start this chapter by acknowledging the research that has shown only 7 percent of communication to be conveyed through words.[11] Seven percent. That is a sobering percentage. Despite that low percentage, I am convinced that the more careful we are with the words we use, the more effective we will be—certainly in written communication where all we have are words. The other side of this is that the words we choose to use affect how we think about things and whether we will have an optimistic or pessimistic outlook on ourselves, our work, and our lives. Some call it positive self-talk. Here are some words and phrases I suggest not using along with their more productive alternatives.

Hope versus Expect. "I hope to have the final $100,000 committed to by May." The more productive alternative would be: "I expect to have the final $100,000 committed

11. Dr. Albert Mehrabian, author of *Silent Messages*.

to by May." Expect good things to happen. Expect to succeed.

Just. "I was just calling to see if you are open for a visit." This word is often used when we're afraid the person we are talking to will be offended or bothered by the request. You have something very important to speak with your donors about. There is no need to be apologetic. Say instead, "I was calling to see if you are open for a visit." You will sound just as polite but much more sure of yourself.

I want. "I want to come out and visit with you." Newsflash! No one cares what you want. How about: you might find it helpful, you might enjoy, or you might be interested in visiting?

Sorry. "Sorry it took me so long to get back to you." Instead, try: "Thanks for your patience in my getting back to you." It's more positive and less self-deprecating. When you make a mistake, instead of saying "I am sorry," say "I apologize." According to diffen.com:

> An apology is a formal admission of a wrongdoing. It may or may not be heartfelt—i.e., a person may apologize without feeling remorseful. On the other hand, saying "I am sorry" is usually seen as being a truer admission of regret. It is what is called a "heartfelt apology." If someone says he is sorry but does not feel any remorse, then he is said to be lying.

Would. Would you be prepared, or would you consider (making a gift, including us in your will, etc.)? Instead, say:

"Are you prepared to" or "will you consider?" It's more intentional and action-oriented.

But. We all know this negates whatever we said before it. Use "and." For example: "I appreciate your commitment to making a gift to athletics, and it might have more of an impact if we adjust a few things. Are you open to exploring some ideas?"

I am not sure. This one is a little tricky. Have you ever found yourself saying to a donor, "I am not sure how you feel about (fill in the blank)" and then you continue to talk without asking them how they felt? I catch myself doing that occasionally, and have to stop and ask the donor, "Well, can you tell me how you feel about _____?" (Rather than guessing.)

Seven Most Powerful Words to Persuade People

(Disclaimer: "Persuade" has a bad connotation. If the donor is interested in doing more and we are offering an appropriate solution, it's perfectly acceptable to persuade the donor to take action.)

Here are the seven most powerful words to persuade people as identified by Michael Hartzell,[12] along with my ideas on how to adapt them to fundraising.

Because. Professor and psychologist Dr. Robert Cialdini has dedicated his life to understanding and teaching human persuasion. He performed some experiments using the word "because." When people requesting a favor

---

12. Michael Hartzell, https://www.michaelhartzell.com/Blog/bid/92824/The-Seven-Most-Powerful-Words-to-Persuade

used the word "because," their favorable response rate rose significantly. It's a subtle thing that is easy enough to use. I use "because" whenever possible. For example: "John, I am calling to set up a time for us to visit because..."

Now. This is a great way to create an appropriate sense of urgency. "Please consider making a gift now."

Imagine. "Imagine a world where all kids can live a productive life. Imagine the impact we can have with every board member making a significant gift."

Please. "Please consider increasing your commitment to help us find a cure."

Thank you. "Thank you for your continued support. Thank you for all you do."

The person's name. Use the donor's name whenever possible, but don't overdo it.

Words that indicate they are in **control.** These are great for seniors. According to author David Solie, one of the biggest concerns seniors have is losing control. If you can help donors stay in control, you'll build trust faster and strengthen your relationships. Staying in control means it's their decision to choose what they want to accomplish for themselves, their family, and the impact they want to have on the people we serve. Examples include:

- "Take control of your estate."
- "You decide."

- "What do you want to accomplish on our visit today?"

Check out David Solie's book *How to Say It to Seniors*.

 IF YOU REMEMBER NOTHING ELSE:

✓ Think about the words you are using in your written communication and voicemails.

✓ Use words that influence people.

CHAPTER 28:

FOLLOW UP AND FOLLOW THROUGH

This is my favorite chapter, because the subject is deceptively simple yet is so often taken for granted—following up and following through. I worked with my father, Ben, for fifteen years. He ran a small, successful print sales business. Ben did really well. Not because he was a smooth talker—in fact, he was not your typical salesman. He was a quiet man. He earned people's trust quickly. From day one of working with him, he taught me that even if I lacked the years of experience that our competitors had, and even if I did not have the advanced training, if I just kept showing up on people's doorsteps, eventually they would give me a chance. Why? Because most salespeople give up after one or two attempts.

There is a great story from one of my favorite motivational speakers, Les Brown. I heard him tell it many years ago, but I still think of it often. At a young age, Les badly wanted to be a radio DJ. This was back in the 1970s when radio disc jockeys were celebrities. One day, he rustled up the courage to go down to his local radio station and ask for a job. The owner of the station immediately kicked Les out. Les was determined. He went back the next day asking for a job all over again. The owner screamed, "Weren't you here yesterday, and didn't I tell you there are no jobs here?" Les replied with "Yes, but that was yesterday. Things always change." (I love that attitude.) Weeks went by and Les kept showing up, only to be turned away every time. Finally, after several months of doing this, the owner looked at him, impressed by Les's persistence, and said, "Okay, well, go get me a cup of coffee." Les started as a maintenance guy, but he longed to get behind that microphone. One night, it was just Les and the DJ doing his show. Lucky for Les, the DJ was known to hit the sauce while on air. This night, the DJ was hitting it so hard he passed out. Les seized the opportunity, ran into the DJ booth, and took over. This was the beginning of a great career in radio that led Les to a successful speaking career.

He had very little education and no experience, but he kept showing up to make sure he was there at the right time. As I wrote earlier in this book, I am a huge believer in training, reading, and studying our craft—being the eternal student. I have worked with several people who had practically no experience in fundraising yet who could go out and close gifts because they kept showing up.

Think of people you deal with in your own life. It can be personally or professionally. Look at how many times people say they will do something, yet there is no follow-up. I see it a lot. I am not trying to say these people are wrong. Most people, certainly in fundraising, have the best intentions. Several times a month, I will speak with or meet with someone—not a client or donor, but someone whom I have offered to help find a job or introduce to a potential new client. I continue to be amazed at the percentage of people who never follow through. Everyone is busy. The takeaway for me is, if I work hard and focus on being good at follow-up, I am more likely to get what I am looking for. When I am cultivating a donor, and I know the donor is working with fundraisers from other charities, I remind myself that not everyone is good at following up, and if I keep showing up and doing what I say I will do, my organization is more likely to get a larger share of the donor's charitable giving. I am not saying I am better than anyone. I do, however, work very hard at being the best at following up that I can be.

Here are a few simple ways to be a master follow-upper:

- Ask the donor how you should follow up. When a donor says to stay in touch, what does that mean? Ask them. "How should I follow up? When and how often should I check in?" Let them feel that they are in control of the relationship, not you.

- When someone refers you to a friend, client, or colleague, follow up with that person to let him or her know when you connect with the contact. Then let your person know what ultimately happens because of the introduction. It drives me crazy when I take the time to make an introduction for someone and I never hear back as to whether he or she even took the first step to call the person. I am thrilled to make introductions, but don't like wasting time if the person never bothers to follow through. It also gives me satisfaction to know that I helped someone with a simple gesture of an introduction.

- Send a handwritten thank-you note. When someone buys you lunch or does something nice for you, send a handwritten note. It's a rare thing these days to get a note like that in the mail. You will stand out from the rest of the pack, I promise you.

- Set a follow-up appointment right away. How many times have you spent valuable time with someone, had a good conversation, yet you never hear from them again? If you are meeting with someone and there is nothing urgent to follow up on, but you all agree to stay in touch, before you leave that meeting, have everyone get out his or her calendar and set a future date to check in. This will keep the person at the top of your mind.

IF YOU REMEMBER NOTHING ELSE:

✓ Sometimes the gifts go to those who do the best job of following up.

CHAPTER 29:

PICK UP THE CHECK

Years ago, I was doing some personal fundraising for a non-profit I cared about very much. They are a big organization. The money I was raising would have felt like a much larger gift to a smaller organization. My share of the donation was one of the largest outright gifts I had ever made. I was working with a fundraiser whose office was about thirty miles from my home. The fundraiser was a really nice guy and very good at what he did. One day, I gathered the first pile of checks I had collected. They totaled about $15,000. I let the fundraiser know that I wanted to get them to him, but I did not want to spend the time fighting traffic to get downtown and would mail them. He did not offer to pick them up.

After further thought, I worried about the checks never getting there and having to go back to tell all my donors that their checks had been lost. The next day, I was on the road in another town and decided to find a post office to send the checks by express mail. The process took me close to an hour. It took me a while to find a parking space (which

I had to pay for), then I had to wait in line at the post office. Then the required forms took a while to fill out. And it cost me $15 to mail it. As I got back in my car, I wondered why I, as the donor, was going through all that work when the fundraiser could have offered to pick up the checks. I am not trying to make out that the fundraiser was wrong. I was a small fish in a big pond, but that did not mean I would always be a small fish. I could have grown into a loyal longtime donor. Take every opportunity to go see a donor, especially if they want to make a donation. Every chance I get, I will offer to pick up a check from the donor. Most tell me no thanks, but the very gesture of offering lets donors know they are special and I am willing to go the extra mile(s) to make it easier for them. Go out of your way and take advantage of every opportunity to go see donors.

Over and over again, fundraisers tell me that the activity they enjoy most in their work is getting out to see donors. You can increase that time. Be intentional, make the right choices, and keep putting it out there. Remember: Some Will, Some Won't, So What, Someone's Waiting.

IF YOU REMEMBER NOTHING ELSE:

✓ Make it easy for donors to "do business with you."

✓ Ask donors how you can improve your customer (donor) service.

✓ Take advantage of every opportunity to visit your donors.

CHAPTER 30:

A THANK YOU WOULD BE NICE

I went to see a medical specialist for an annoying and persistent medical challenge I was having. In this day of skyrocketing healthcare costs and overworked doctors and nurses, I was blown away by my experience with this specialist. When I arrived, the receptionist introduced herself and thanked me for coming in. The doctor was running fifteen minutes late, and the receptionist checked in with me several times to see if I needed anything. I was then greeted by a medical assistant who introduced himself, shook my hand, and gave me his card, telling me to give him a call if I ever needed anything. When the doctor came in, he apologized profusely for being fifteen minutes late. After my first visit, I received a handwritten note from the receptionist—yes, the receptionist—thanking me for coming in. I also received a signed letter from the doctor, thanking me for my business. A week later, I received a voicemail from the office checking in to see how I was feeling. I have not experienced anything like that in healthcare before or since. It got me thinking about the experience we create for our donors, for the first-time givers and the long-time givers. It's common knowledge that our next gift is most likely to come from our past donors, yet the attrition rate of donors nationally is over 50 percent. I am convinced it's due to lack of proper thanking and stewardship.

I would like to share my perspective as a donor toward how I like to be stewarded. The key to proper stewardship is consistency, personalization, and constant contact. Here is a short list of ways to provide amazing stewardship:

- Pick up the phone and thank all your donors for their first-time gift. With the popularity of e-mails, people have gotten away from that.

- Once a donor has been giving for ten years, send them a thank-you card and give them a call. Consider creating a true-blue society to honor long-time donors. These are great planned giving prospects.

- Call as many donors as you can on their birthdays and remind them how much you appreciate them.

- When sending an e-mail or a note card to a donor, end your message with "I (or we) appreciate you."

- Have someone from your organization who benefits from gifts (student, nurse, client, actor, etc.) call donors just to say "Thanks, we cannot do what we do without people like you."

- Assign a handful of medium-level donors to all of your board members at your next donor event. Task the board members with introducing themselves to their assigned donors, thanking the donors for all they do. I cannot tell you how many donor events my wife and I have gone to where most trustees ignored us.

- Have a written policy (especially for planned giving) that lays out in detail how you will acknowledge and thank donors.

 IF YOU REMEMBER NOTHING ELSE:

✓ We donors never get thanked enough.

✓ Ask your donors how they would like to be thanked.

CHAPTER 31:
FINAL THOUGHTS

"Do what you can, with what you have, where you are."

– Theodore Roosevelt

Technology is evolving at breakneck speeds. A new generation of donors is changing the way we raise money. No matter how much people change, no matter how the ways they live their lives and make decisions evolve, one thing will never change (at least not in our lifetime): the need and desire to connect with people on a one-to-one basis.

Relationships are best developed by spending more time with our donors. Look at where your largest gifts are coming from. Most likely, it's not through online giving, text giving, or direct mail. Few things will take the place of raising significant gifts face-to-face with donors.

Now more than ever, our success depends on spending quality time with the right donors. Continually improving your mindset, your behavior, and your skillsets will make that happen.

You work hard, you work long hours, and you make many sacrifices. You change lives, and you leave your legacy. I wish you all the best on your journey.

Now Go See People!

Joseph Tumolo, CAP®

 Joe uses a tested and proven methodology he developed to help fundraisers and organizations build thriving and sustaining major and planned giving programs. Joe trains fundraisers to move away from transactional fundraising and toward building relationships that lead to deeper and longer lasting relationships with donors. Those relationships lead to more engaged donors and more planned gifts.

Joe has an Associate's degree from Montgomery County Community College and a Bachelor's of Science from Saint Joseph's University in Philadelphia. He received his Chartered Advisor in Philanthropy certification from the American College in Bryn Mawr, PA. He lives in the Philadelphia area with his wife Lorraine and the Jack Russell/hound dog they rescued, Tye.

We need to focus on what's most important— building relationships with our donors

Joe Tumolo
joetumolo.com

Major and Planned Gifts Training
Coaching
Speaking

We can help with:

- Planned Giving Program Development
- Major Gifts Training
- Board Presentations
- Development Retreats
- Speaking

Contact Joe today at (610) 653-7906 to receive a FREE Basic Needs Assessment for your organization and learn how you can take your program to the next level by keeping it SIMPLE.

Visit him online at www.joetumolo.com